THE POEMS OF

WILLIAM WATSON

THE POEMS OF

WILLIAM WATSON

NEW EDITION

REARRANGED BY THE AUTHOR

WITH ADDITIONS

New York

MACMILLAN AND CO.

AND LONDON

1893

Norwood Press:
J. S. Cushing & Co. — Berwick & Smith.
Boston, Mass., U.S.A.

CONTENTS

CONTENTS.

ELEGIAC POEMS

WORDSWORTH'S GRAVE

TO JAMES BROMLEY

With "Wordsworth's Grave"

Ere vandal lords with lust of gold accurst
   Deface each hallowed hillside we revere —
Ere cities in their million-throated thirst
   Menace each sacred mere —
Let us give thanks because one nook hath been
   Unflooded yet by desecration's wave,
The little churchyard in the valley green
   That holds our Wordsworth's grave.

'Twas there I plucked these elegiac blooms,
   There where he rests 'mid comrades fit and few,
And thence I bring this growth of classic tombs,
   An offering, friend, to you —
You who have loved like me his simple themes,
   Loved his sincere large accent nobly plain,
And loved the land whose mountains and whose
     streams
   Are lovelier for his strain.

5

It may be that his manly chant, beside
    More dainty numbers, seems a rustic tune ;
It may be, thought has broadened since he died
    Upon the century's noon ;
It may be that we can no longer share
    The faith which from his fathers he received ;
It may be that our doom is to despair
    Where he with joy believed ; —

Enough that there is none since risen who sings
    A song so gotten of the immediate soul,
So instant from the vital fount of things
    Which is our source and goal ;
And though at touch of later hands there float
    More artful tones than from his lyre he drew,
Ages may pass ere trills another note
    So sweet, so great, so true.

WORDSWORTH'S GRAVE

I

THE old rude church, with bare, bald tower, is here ;
  Beneath its shadow high-born Rotha flows ;
Rotha, remembering well who slumbers near,
  And with cool murmur lulling his repose.

Rotha, remembering well who slumbers near.
  His hills, his lakes, his streams are with him yet.
Surely the heart that read her own heart clear
  Nature forgets not soon : 'tis we forget.

We that with vagrant soul his fixity
  Have slighted ; faithless, done his deep faith wrong ;
Left him for poorer loves, and bowed the knee
  To misbegotten strange new gods of song.

Yet, led by hollow ghost or beckoning elf
  Far from her homestead to the desert bourn,
The vagrant soul returning to herself
  Wearily wise, must needs to him return.

To him and to the powers that with him dwell : —
 Inflowings that divulged not whence they came ;
And that secluded spirit unknowable,
 The mystery we make darker with a name ;

The Somewhat which we name but cannot know,
 Ev'n as we name a star and only see
His quenchless flashings forth, which ever show
 And ever hide him, and which are not he.

II

Poet who sleepest by this wandering wave !
 When thou wast born, what birth-gift hadst thou then ?.
To thee what wealth was that the Immortals gave,
 The wealth thou gavest in thy turn to men?

Not Milton's keen, translunar music thine ;
 Not Shakespeare's cloudless, boundless human view ;
Not Shelley's flush of rose on peaks divine ;
 Nor yet the wizard twilight Coleridge knew.

What hadst thou that could make so large amends
 For all thou hadst not and thy peers possessed,
Motion and fire, swift means to radiant ends? —
 Thou hadst, for weary feet, the gift of rest.

From Shelley's dazzling glow or thunderous haze,
   From Byron's tempest-anger, tempest-mirth,
Men turned to thee and found — not blast and blaze,
   Tumult of tottering heavens, but peace on earth.

Nor peace that grows by Lethe, scentless flower,
   There in white languors to decline and cease ;
But peace whose names are also rapture, power,
   Clear sight, and love : for these are parts of peace.

III

I hear it vouched the Muse is with us still ; —
   If less divinely frenzied than of yore,
In lieu of feelings she has wondrous skill
   To simulate emotion felt no more.

Not such the authentic Presence pure, that made
   This valley vocal in the great days gone ! —
In *his* great days, while yet the spring-time played
   About him, and the mighty morning shone.

No word-mosaic artificer, he sang
   A lofty song of lowly weal and dole.
Right from the heart, right to the heart it sprang,
   Or from the soul leapt instant to the soul.

He felt the charm of childhood, grace of youth,
    Grandeur of age, insisting to be sung.
The impassioned argument was simple truth
    Half-wondering at its own melodious tongue.

Impassioned? ay, to the song's ecstatic core !
    But far removed were clangour, storm and feud ;
For plenteous health was his, exceeding store
    Of joy, and an impassioned quietude.

IV

A hundred years ere he to manhood came,
    Song from celestial heights had wandered down,
Put off her robe of sunlight, dew and flame,
    And donned a modish dress to charm the Town.

Thenceforth she but festooned the porch of things ;
    Apt at life's lore, incurious what life meant.
Dextrous of hand, she struck her lute's few strings ;
    Ignobly perfect, barrenly content.

Unflushed with ardour and unblanched with awe,
    Her lips in profitless derision curled,
She saw with dull emotion — if she saw —
    The vision of the glory of the world.

The human masque she watched, with dreamless eyes
   In whose clear shallows lurked no trembling shade :
The stars, unkenned by her, might set and rise,
   Unmarked by her, the daisies bloom and fade.

The age grew sated with her sterile wit.
   Herself waxed weary on her loveless throne.
Men felt life's tide, the sweep and surge of it,
   And craved a living voice, a natural tone.

For none the less, though song was but half true,
   The world lay common, one abounding theme.
Man joyed and wept, and fate was ever new,
   And love was sweet, life real, death no dream.

In sad stern verse the rugged scholar-sage
   Bemoaned his toil unvalued, youth uncheered.
His numbers wore the vesture of the age,
   But, 'neath it beating, the great heart was heard.

From dewy pastures, uplands sweet with thyme,
   A virgin breeze freshened the jaded day.
It wafted Collins' lonely vesper-chime,
   It breathed abroad the frugal note of Gray.

It fluttered here and there, nor swept in vain
  The dusty haunts where futile echoes dwell, —
Then, in a cadence soft as summer rain,
  And sad from Auburn voiceless, drooped and fell.

It drooped and fell, and one 'neath northern skies,
  With southern heart, who tilled his father's field,
Found Poesy a-dying, bade her rise
  And touch quick nature's hem and go forth healed.

On life's broad plain the ploughman's conquering share
  Upturned the fallow lands of truth anew,
And o'er the formal garden's trim parterre
  The peasant's team a ruthless furrow drew.

Bright was his going forth, but clouds ere long
  Whelmed him ; in gloom his radiance set, and those
Twin morning stars of the new century's song,
  Those morning stars that sang together, rose.

In elvish speech the *Dreamer* told his tale
  Of marvellous oceans swept by fateful wings. —
The *Seër* strayed not from earth's human pale,
  But the mysterious face of common things

He mirrored as the moon in Rydal Mere
   Is mirrored, when the breathless night hangs blue :
Strangely remote she seems and wondrous near,
   And by some nameless difference born anew.

V

Peace — peace — and rest !   Ah, how the lyre is loth,
   Or powerless now, to give what all men seek !
Either it deadens with ignoble sloth
   Or deafens with shrill tumult, loudly weak.

Where is the singer whose large notes and clear
   Can heal and arm and plenish and sustain ?
Lo, one with empty music floods the ear,
   And one, the heart refreshing, tires the brain.

And idly tuneful, the loquacious throng
   Flutter and twitter, prodigal of time,
And little masters make a toy of song
   Till grave men weary of the sound of rhyme.

And some go prankt in faded antique dress,
   Abhorring to be hale and glad and free ;
And some parade a conscious naturalness,
   The scholar's not the child's simplicity.

Enough ; — and wisest who from words forbear.
  The kindly river rails not as it glides ;
And suave and charitable, the winning air
  Chides not at all, or only him who chides.

VI

Nature ! we storm thine ear with choric notes.
  Thou answerest through the calm great nights and
      days,
" Laud me who will : not tuneless are your throats ;
  Yet if ye paused I should not miss the praise."

We falter, half-rebuked, and sing again.
  We chant thy desertness and haggard gloom,
Or with thy splendid wrath inflate the strain,
  Or touch it with thy colour and perfume.

One, his melodious blood aflame for thee,
  Wooed with fierce lust, his hot heart world-defiled.
One, with the upward eye of infancy,
  Looked in thy face, and felt himself thy child.

Thee he approached without distrust or dread —
  Beheld thee throned, an awful queen, above —
Climbed to thy lap and merely laid his head
  Against thy warm wild heart of mother-love.

He heard that vast heart beating — thou didst press
    Thy child so close, and lov'dst him unaware.
Thy beauty gladdened him ; yet he scarce less
    Had loved thee, had he never found thee fair !

For thou wast not as legendary lands
    To which with curious eyes and ears we roam.
Nor wast thou as a fane mid solemn sands,
    Where palmers halt at evening.   Thou wast home.

And here, at home, still bides he ; but he sleeps ;
    Not to be wakened even at thy word ;
Though we, vague dreamers, dream he somewhere keeps
    An ear still open to thy voice still heard, —

Thy voice, as heretofore, about him blown,
    For ever blown about his silence now ;
Thy voice, though deeper, yet so like his own
    That almost, when he sang, we deemed 'twas thou !

VII

Behind Helm Crag and Silver Howe the sheen
    Of the retreating day is less and less.
Soon will the lordlier summits, here unseen,
    Gather the night about their nakedness.

The half-heard bleat of sheep comes from the hill,
　　Faint sounds of childish play are in the air.
The river murmurs past.　All else is still.
　　The very graves seem stiller than they were.

Afar though nation be on nation hurled,
　　And life with toil and ancient pain depressed,
Here one may scarce believe the whole wide world
　　Is not at peace, and all man's heart at rest.

Rest !　'twas the gift *he* gave ; and peace ! the shade
　　He spread, for spirits fevered with the sun.
To him his bounties are come back — here laid
　　In rest, in peace, his labour nobly done.

SHELLEY'S CENTENARY

(4TH AUGUST 1892)

WITHIN a narrow span of time,
Three princes of the realm of rhyme,
At height of youth or manhood's prime,
    From earth took wing,
To join the fellowship sublime
    Who, dead, yet sing.

He, first, his earliest wreath who wove
Of laurel grown in Latmian grove,
Conquered by pain and hapless love
    Found calmer home,
Roofed by the heaven that glows above
    Eternal Rome.

A fierier soul, its own fierce prey,
And cumbered with more mortal clay,
At Missolonghi flamed away,
    And left the air
Reverberating to this day
    Its loud despair.

Alike remote from Byron's scorn,
And Keats's magic as of morn
Bursting for ever newly-born
    On forests old,
Waking a hoary world forlorn
    With touch of gold,

Shelley, the cloud-begot, who grew
Nourished on air and sun and dew,
Into that Essence whence he drew
    His life and lyre
Was fittingly resolved anew
    Through wave and fire.

'Twas like his rapid soul !　'Twas meet
That he, who brooked not Time's slow feet,
With passage thus abrupt and fleet
    Should hurry hence,
Eager the Great Perhaps to greet
    With Why? and Whence?

Impatient of the world's fixed way,
He ne'er could suffer God's delay,
But all the future in a day
    Would build divine,
And the whole past in ruins lay,
    An emptied shrine.

Vain vision ! but the glow, the fire,
The passion of benign desire,
The glorious yearning, lift him higher
    Than many a soul
That mounts a million paces nigher
    Its meaner goal.

And power is his, if naught besides,
In that thin ether where he rides,
Above the roar of human tides
    To ascend afar,
Lost in a storm of light that hides
    His dizzy car.

Below, the unhastening world toils on,
And here and there are victories won,
Some dragon slain, some justice done,
    While, through the skies,
A meteor rushing on the sun,
    He flares and dies.

But, as he cleaves yon ether clear
Notes from the unattempted Sphere
He scatters to the enchanted ear
    Of earth's dim throng,
Whose dissonance doth more endear
    The showering song.

In other shapes than he forecast
The world is moulded : his fierce blast, —
His wild assault upon the Past, —
    These things are vain ;
Revolt is transient : what *must* last
    Is that pure strain,

Which seems the wandering voices blent
Of every virgin element, —
A sound from ocean caverns sent, —
    An airy call
From the pavilioned firmament
    O'erdoming all.

And in this world of worldlings, where
Souls rust in apathy, and ne'er
A great emotion shakes the air,
    And life flags tame,
And rare is noble impulse, rare
    The impassioned aim,

'Tis no mean fortune to have heard
A singer who, if errors blurred
His sight, had yet a spirit stirred
    By vast desire,
And ardour fledging the swift word
    With plumes of fire.

A creature of impetuous breath,
Our torpor deadlier than death
He knew not ; whatsoe'er he saith
 Flashes with life :
He spurreth men, he quickeneth
 To splendid strife.

And in his gusts of song he brings
Wild odours shaken from strange wings,
And unfamiliar whisperings
 From far lips blown,
While all the rapturous heart of things
 Throbs through his own, —

His own that from the burning pyre
One who had loved his wind-swept lyre
Out of the sharp teeth of the fire
 Unmolten drew,
Beside the sea that in her ire
 Smote him and slew.

IN LALEHAM CHURCHYARD

(August 18, 1890)

'Twas at this season, year by year,
The singer who lies songless here
Was wont to woo a less austere,
　　　Less deep repose,
Where Rotha to Winandermere
　　　Unresting flows, —

Flows through a land where torrents call
To far-off torrents as they fall,
And mountains in their cloudy pall
　　　Keep ghostly state,
And Nature makes majestical
　　　Man's lowliest fate.

There, 'mid the August glow, still came
He of the twice-illustrious name,
The loud impertinence of fame

    Not loth to flee —
Not loth with brooks and fells to claim
    Fraternity.

Linked with his happy youthful lot,
Is Loughrigg, then, at last forgot?
Nor silent peak nor dalesman's cot
    Looks on his grave.
Lulled by the Thames he sleeps, and not
    By Rotha's wave.

'Tis fittest thus ! for though with skill
He sang of beck and tarn and ghyll,
The deep, authentic mountain-thrill
    Ne'er shook his page !
Somewhat of worldling mingled still
    With bard and sage.

And 'twere less meet for him to lie
Guarded by summits lone and high
That traffic with the eternal sky
    And hear, unawed,
The everlasting fingers ply
    The loom of God,

Than, in this hamlet of the plain,
A less sublime repose to gain,
Where Nature, genial and urbane,
 To man defers,
Yielding to us the right to reign,
 Which yet is hers.

And nigh to where his bones abide,
The Thames with its unruffled tide
Seems like his genius typified, —
 Its strength, its grace,
Its lucid gleam, its sober pride,
 Its tranquil pace.

But ah ! not his the eventual fate
Which doth the journeying wave await —
Doomed to resign its limpid state
 And quickly grow
Turbid as passion, dark as hate,
 And wide as woe.

Rather, it may be, over-much
He shunned the common stain and smutch,
From soilure of ignoble touch

Too grandly free,
Too loftily secure in such
Cold purity.

But he preserved from chance control
The fortress of his 'stablisht soul;
In all things sought to see the Whole;
Brooked no disguise;
And set his heart upon the goal,
Not on the prize.

With those Elect he shall survive
Who seem not to compete or strive,
Yet with the foremost still arrive,
Prevailing still:
Spirits with whom the stars connive
To work their will.

And ye, the baffled many, who,
Dejected, from afar off view
The easily victorious few
Of calm renown, —
Have ye not your sad glory too,
And mournful crown?

Great is the facile conqueror;
Yet haply he, who, wounded sore,
Breathless, unhorsed, all covered o'er
    With blood and sweat,
Sinks foiled, but fighting evermore, —
    Is greater yet.

LACHRYMÆ MUSARUM

(6TH OCTOBER 1892)

Low, like another's, lies the laurelled head :
The life that seemed a perfect song is o'er :
Carry the last great bard to his last bed.
Land that he loved, thy noblest voice is mute.
Land that he loved, that loved him ! nevermore
Meadow of thine, smooth lawn or wild sea-shore,
Gardens of odorous bloom and tremulous fruit,
Or woodlands old, like Druid couches spread,
The master's feet shall tread.
Death's little rift hath rent the faultless lute :
The singer of undying songs is dead.

  Lo, in this season pensive-hued and grave,
While fades and falls the doomed, reluctant leaf
From withered Earth's fantastic coronal,
With wandering sighs of forest and of wave
Mingles the murmur of a people's grief
For him whose leaf shall fade not, neither fall.

He hath fared forth, beyond these suns and showers.
For us, the autumn glow, the autumn flame,
And soon the winter silence shall be ours :
Him the eternal spring of fadeless fame
Crowns with no mortal flowers.

Rapt though he be from us,
Virgil salutes him, and Theocritus ;
Catullus, mightiest-brained Lucretius, each
Greets him, their brother, on the Stygian beach ;
Proudly a gaunt right hand doth Dante reach ;
Milton and Wordsworth bid him welcome home ;
Bright Keats to touch his raiment doth beseech ;
Coleridge, his locks aspersed with fairy foam,
Calm Spenser, Chaucer suave,
His equal friendship crave :
And godlike spirits hail him guest, in speech
Of Athens, Florence, Weimar, Stratford, Rome.

What needs his laurel our ephemeral tears,
To save from visitation of decay?
Not in this temporal sunlight, now, that bay
Blooms, nor to perishable mundane ears
Sings he with lips of transitory clay ;
For he hath joined the chorus of his peers
In habitations of the perfect day :

His earthly notes a heavenly audience hears,
And more melodious are henceforth the spheres,
Enriched with music stol'n from earth away.

He hath returned to regions whence he came.
Him doth the spirit divine
Of universal loveliness reclaim.
All nature is his shrine.
Seek him henceforward in the wind and sea,
In earth's and air's emotion or repose,
In every star's august serenity,
And in the rapture of the flaming rose.
There seek him if ye would not seek in vain,
There, in the rhythm and music of the Whole ;
Yea, and for ever in the human soul
Made stronger and more beauteous by his strain.

For lo ! creation's self is one great choir,
And what is nature's order but the rhyme
Whereto the worlds keep time,
And all things move with all things from their prime?
Who shall expound the mystery of the lyre?
In far retreats of elemental mind
Obscurely comes and goes
The imperative breath of song, that as the wind
Is trackless, and oblivious whence it blows.

Demand of lilies wherefore they are white,
Extort her crimson secret from the rose,
But ask not of the Muse that she disclose
The meaning of the riddle of her might :
Somewhat of all things sealed and recondite,
Save the enigma of herself, she knows.
The master could not tell, with all his lore,
Wherefore he sang, or whence the mandate sped :
Ev'n as the linnet sings, so I, he said ; —
Ah, rather as the imperial nightingale,
That held in trance the ancient Attic shore,
And charms the ages with the notes that o'er
All woodland chants immortally prevail !
And now, from our vain plaudits greatly fled,
He with diviner silence dwells instead,
And on no earthly sea with transient roar,
Unto no earthly airs, he trims his sail,
But far beyond our vision and our hail
Is heard for ever and is seen no more.

No more, O never now,
Lord of the lofty and the tranquil brow
Whereon nor snows of time
Have fall'n, nor wintry rime,
Shall men behold thee, sage and mage sublime.
Once, in his youth obscure,

The maker of this verse, which shall endure
By splendour of its theme that cannot die,
Beheld thee eye to eye,
And touched through thee the hand
Of every hero of thy race divine,
Ev'n to the sire of all the laurelled line,
The sightless wanderer on the Ionian strand,
With soul as healthful as the poignant brine,
Wide as his skies and radiant as his seas,
Starry from haunts of his Familiars nine,
Glorious Mæonides.
Yea, I beheld thee, and behold thee yet :
Thou hast forgotten, but can I forget?
The accents of thy pure and sovereign tongue,
Are they not ever goldenly impressed
On memory's palimpsest?
I see the wizard locks like night that hung,
I tread the floor thy hallowing feet have trod ;
I see the hands a nation's lyre that strung,
The eyes that looked through life and gazed on God.

The seasons change, the winds they shift and veer ;
The grass of yesteryear
Is dead ; the birds depart, the groves decay :
Empires dissolve and peoples disappear :
Song passes not away.

Captains and conquerors leave a little dust,
And kings a dubious legend of their reign ;
The swords of Cæsars, they are less than rust :
The poet doth remain.
Dead is Augustus, Maro is alive ;
And thou, the Mantuan of our age and clime,
Like Virgil shalt thy race and tongue survive,
Bequeathing no less honeyed words to time,
Embalmed in amber of eternal rhyme,
And rich with sweets from every Muse's hive ;
While to the measure of the cosmic rune
For purer ears thou shalt thy lyre attune,
And heed no more the hum of idle praise
In that great calm our tumults cannot reach,
Master who crown'st our immelodious days
With flower of perfect speech.

EPIGRAMS

EPIGRAMS

'Tis human fortune's happiest height to be
   A spirit melodious, lucid, poised, and whole ;
Second in order of felicity
   I hold it, to have walk'd with such a soul.

The statue — Buonarroti said — doth wait,
Thrall'd in the block, for me to emancipate.
The poem — saith the poet — wanders free
Till I betray it to captivity.

To keep in sight Perfection, and adore
   The vision, is the artist's best delight ;
His bitterest pang, that he can ne'er do more
   Than keep her long'd-for loveliness in sight.

If Nature be a phantasm, as thou say'st,
　　A splendid fiction and prodigious dream,
To reach the real and true I'll make no haste,
　　More than content with worlds that only seem.

The Poet gathers fruit from every tree,
Yea, grapes from thorns and figs from thistles he.
Pluck'd by his hand, the basest weed that grows
Towers to a lily, reddens to a rose.

Brook, from whose bridge the wandering idler peers
　　To watch thy small fish dart or cool floor shine,
I would that bridge whose arches all are years
　　Spann'd not a less transparent wave than thine !

To Art we go as to a well, athirst,
　　And see our shadow 'gainst its mimic skies,
But in its depth must plunge and be immersed
　　To clasp the naiad Truth where low she lies.

In youth the artist voweth lover's vows
To Art, in manhood maketh her his spouse.
Well if her charms yet hold for him such joy
As when he craved some boon and she was coy !

IMMURED in sense, with fivefold bonds confined,
  Rest we content if whispers from the stars
In waftings of the incalculable wind
  Come blown at midnight through our prison-bars.

LOVE, like a bird, hath perch'd upon a spray
  For thee and me to hearken what he sings.
Contented, he forgets to fly away ;
  But hush ! . . . remind not Eros of his wings.

THINK not thy wisdom can illume away
The ancient tanglement of night and day.
Enough, to acknowledge both, and both revere :
They see not clearliest who see all things clear.

IN mid whirl of the dance of Time ye start,
  Start at the cold touch of Eternity,
And cast your cloaks about you, and depart :
  The minstrels pause not in their minstrelsy.

THE beasts in field are glad, and have not wit
  To know why leapt their hearts when springtime shone.
Man looks at his own bliss, considers it,
  Weighs it with curious fingers ; and 'tis gone.

MOMENTOUS to himself as I to me
    Hath each man been that ever woman bore ;
Once, in a lightning-flash of sympathy,
    I *felt* this truth, an instant, and no more.

THE gods man makes he breaks ; proclaims them each
    Immortal, and himself outlives them all :
But whom he set not up he cannot reach
    To shake His cloud-dark sun-bright pedestal.

THE children romp within the graveyard's pale ;
The lark sings o'er a madhouse, or a gaol ; —
Such nice antitheses of perfect poise
Chance in her curious rhetoric employs.

OUR lithe thoughts gambol close to God's abyss,
Children whose home is by the precipice.
Fear not thy little ones shall o'er it fall :
Solid, though viewless, is the girdling wall.

LIVES there whom pain hath evermore pass'd by
And Sorrow shunn'd with an averted eye ?
Him do thou pity, him above the rest,
Him of all hapless mortals most unbless'd.

SAY what thou wilt, the young are happy never.
Give me bless'd Age, beyond the fire and fever, —
Past the delight that shatters, hope that stings,
And eager flutt'ring of life's ignorant wings.

ONWARD the chariot of the Untarrying moves ;
   Nor day divulges him nor night conceals ;
Thou hear'st the echo of unreturning hooves
   And thunder of irrevocable wheels.

A DEFT musician does the breeze become
   Whenever an Æolian harp it finds :
Hornpipe and hurdygurdy both are dumb
   Unto the most musicianly of winds.

I FOLLOW Beauty ; of her train am I :
   Beauty whose voice is earth and sea and air ;
Who serveth, and her hands for all things ply ;
   Who reigneth, and her throne is everywhere.

TOILING and yearning, 'tis man's doom to see
   No perfect creature fashion'd of his hands.
Insulted by a flower's immaculacy,
   And mock'd at by the flawless stars he stands.

For metaphors of man we search the skies,
 And find our allegory in all the air.
We gaze on Nature with Narcissus-eyes,
 Enamour'd of our shadow everywhere.

One music maketh its occult abode
 In all things scatter'd from great Beauty's hand ;
And evermore the deepest words of God
 Are yet the easiest to understand.

Enough of mournful melodies, my lute !
Be henceforth joyous, or be henceforth mute.
Song's breath is wasted when it does but fan
The smouldering infelicity of man.

I pluck'd this flower, O brighter flower, for thee,
There where the river dies into the sea.
To kiss it the wild west wind hath made free :
Kiss it thyself and give it back to me.

To be as this old elm full loth were I,
 That shakes in the autumn storm its palsied head.
Hewn by the weird last woodman let me lie
 Ere the path rustle with my foliage shed.

AH, vain, thrice vain in the end, thy hate and rage,
And the shrill tempest of thy clamorous page.
True poets but transcendent lovers be,
And one great love-confession poesy.

———————

HIS rhymes the poet flings at all men's feet,
    And whoso will may trample on his rhymes.
Should Time let die a song that's true and sweet,
    The singer's loss were more than match'd by Time's.

———————

ON LONGFELLOW'S DEATH

No puissant singer he, whose silence grieves
    To-day the great West's tender heart and strong ;
No singer vast of voice : yet one who leaves
    His native air the sweeter for his song.

———————

BYRON THE VOLUPTUARY

Too avid of earth's bliss, he was of those
    Whom Delight flies because they give her chase.
Only the odour of her wild hair blows
    Back in their faces hungering for her face.

ANTONY AT ACTIUM

HE holds a dubious balance : — yet *that* scale,
Whose freight the world is, surely shall prevail?
No ; Cleopatra droppeth into *this*
One counterpoising orient sultry kiss.

ART

THE thousand painful steps at last are trod,
 At last the temple's difficult door we win ;
But perfect on his pedestal, the god
 Freezes us hopeless when we enter in.

KEATS

HE dwelt with the bright gods of elder time,
 On earth and in their cloudy haunts above.
He loved them : and in recompense sublime,
 The gods, alas ! gave him their fatal love.

AFTER READING " TAMBURLAINE THE GREAT "

YOUR Marlowe's page I close, my Shakspere's ope.
 How welcome — after gong and cymbal's din —
The continuity, the long slow slope
 And vast curves of the gradual violin !

Shelley and Harriet Westbrook

A star look'd down from heaven and loved a flower
Grown in earth's garden — loved it for an hour:
Let eyes that trace his orbit in the spheres
Refuse not, to a ruin'd rosebud, tears.

The Play of " King Lear "

Here Love the slain with Love the slayer lies;
   Deep drown'd are both in the same sunless pool.
Up from its depths that mirror thundering skies
   Bubbles the wan mirth of the mirthless Fool.

To a Poet

Time, the extortioner, from richest beauty
Takes heavy toll and wrings rapacious duty.
Austere of feature if thou carve thy rhyme,
Perchance 'twill pay the lesser tax to Time.

The Year's Minstrelsy

Spring, the low prelude of a lordlier song:
   Summer, a music without hint of death:
Autumn, a cadence lingeringly long:
   Winter, a pause; — the Minstrel-Year takes breath.

The Ruined Abbey

Flower-fondled, clasp'd in ivy's close caress,
    It seems allied with Nature, yet apart : —
Of wood's and wave's insensate loveliness
    The glad, sad, tranquil, passionate, human heart.

Michelangelo's " Moses "

The captain's might, and mystery of the seer —
    Remoteness of Jehovah's colloquist,
Nearness of man's heaven-advocate — are here :
    Alone Mount Nebo's harsh foreshadow is miss'd.

The Alps

Adieu, white brows of Europe ! sovereign brows,
    That wear the sunset for a golden tiar.
With me in memory shall your phantoms house
    For ever, whiter than yourselves, and higher.

The Cathedral Spire

It soars like hearts of hapless men who dare
    To sue for gifts the gods refuse to allot ;
Who climb for ever toward they know not where,
    Baffled for ever by they know not what.

An Epitaph

His friends he loved.   His fellest earthly foes —
　Cats — I believe he did but feign to hate.
My hand will miss the insinuated nose,
　Mine eyes the tail that wagg'd contempt at Fate.

The Metropolitan Underground Railway

Here were a goodly place wherein to die ; —
　Grown latterly to sudden change averse,
All violent contrasts fain avoid would I
　On passing from this world into a worse.

To a Seabird

Fain would I have thee barter fates with me, —
Lone loiterer where the shells like jewels be,
Hung on the fringe and frayed hem of the sea.
But no, — 'twere cruel, wild-wing'd Bliss ! to thee.

On Dürer's *Melencolia*

What holds her fixed far eyes nor lets them range ?
Not the strange sea, strange earth, or heav'n more
　　strange ;
But her own phantom dwarfing these great three,
More strange than all, more old than heav'n, earth, sea.

Tantalus

He wooes for ever, with foil'd lips of drouth,
The wave that wearies not to mock his mouth.
'Tis Lethe's ; they alone that tide have quaff'd
Who never thirsted for the oblivious draught.

A Maiden's Epitaph

She dwelt among us till the flowers, 'tis said,
    Grew jealous of her : with precipitate feet,
As loth to wrong them unawares, she fled.
    Earth is less fragrant now, and heaven more sweet.

THE DREAM OF MAN

DEDICATION OF "THE DREAM OF MAN"

To London, My Hostess

City that waitest to be sung, —
    For whom no hand
To mighty strains the lyre hath strung
    In all this land,
Though mightier theme the mightiest ones
    Sang not of old,
The thrice three sisters' godlike sons
    With lips of gold, —
Till greater voice thy greatness sing
    In loftier times,
Suffer an alien muse to bring
    Her votive rhymes.

Yes, alien in thy midst am I,
    Not of thy brood ;
The nursling of a norland sky
    Of rougher mood :

To me, thy tarrying guest, to me,
    'Mid thy loud hum,
Strayed visions of the moor or sea
    Tormenting come.
Above the thunder of the wheels
    That hurry by,
From lapping of lone waves there steals
    A far-sent sigh ;
And many a dream-reared mountain crest
    My feet have trod,
There where thy Minster in the West
    Gropes toward God.
Yet, from thy presence if I go,
    By woodlands deep
Or ocean-fringes, thou, I know,
    Wilt haunt my sleep ;
Thy restless tides of life will foam,
    Still, in my sight ;
Thy imperturbable dark dome
    Will crown my night.

O sea of living waves that roll
    On golden sands,
Or break on tragic reef and shoal
    'Mid fatal lands ;

O forest wrought of living leaves,
  Some filled with Spring,
Where joy life's festal raiment weaves
  And all birds sing, —
Some trampled in the miry ways,
  Or whirled along
By fury of tempestuous days, —
  Take thou my song !

For thou hast scorned not heretofore
  The gifts of rhyme
I dropped, half faltering, at thy door,
  City sublime ;
And though 'tis true I am but guest
  Within thy gate,
Unto thy hands I owe the best
  Awards of fate.
Imperial hostess ! thanks from me
  To thee belong :
O living forest, living sea,
  Take thou my song !

THE DREAM OF MAN

To the eye and the ear of the Dreamer
    This Dream out of darkness flew,
Through the horn or the ivory portal,
    But he wist not which of the two.

It was the Human Spirit,
    Of all men's souls the Soul,
Man the unwearied climber,
    That climbed to the unknown goal.
And up the steps of the ages,
    The difficult steep ascent,
Man the unwearied climber
    Pauseless and dauntless went.
Æons rolled behind him
    With thunder of far retreat,
And still as he strove he conquered
    And laid his foes at his feet.
Inimical powers of nature,
    Tempest and flood and fire,

The spleen of fickle seasons
  That loved to baulk his desire,
The breath of hostile climates,
  The ravage of blight and dearth,
The old unrest that vexes
  The heart of the moody earth,
The genii swift and radiant
  Sabreing heaven with flame,
He, with a keener weapon,
  The sword of his wit, overcame.
Disease and her ravening offspring,
  Pain with the thousand teeth,
He drave into night primeval,
  The nethermost worlds beneath,
Till the Lord of Death, the undying,
  Ev'n Asraël the King,
No more with Furies for heralds
  Came armed with scourge and sting,
But gentle of voice and of visage,
  By calm Age ushered and led,
A guest, serenely featured,
  Entering, woke no dread.
And, as the rolling æons
  Retreated with pomp of sound,
Man's spirit, grown too lordly
  For this mean orb to bound,

By arts in his youth undreamed of
   His terrene fetters broke,
With enterprise ethereal
   Spurning the natal yoke,
And, stung with divine ambition,
   And fired with a glorious greed,
He annexed the stars and the planets
   And peopled them with his seed.

Then said he, " The infinite Scripture
   I have read and interpreted clear,
And searching all worlds I have found not
   My sovereign or my peer.
In what room of the palace of nature
   Resides the invisible God?
For all her doors I have opened,
   And all her floors I have trod.
If greater than I be her tenant,
   Let him answer my challenging call :
Till then I admit no rival,
   But crown myself master of all."
And forth as that word went bruited,
   By Man unto Man were raised
Fanes of devout self-homage,
   Where he who praised was the praised ;

And from vast unto vast of creation
  The new evangel ran,
And an odour of world-wide incense
  Went up from Man unto Man;
Until, on a solemn feast-day,
  When the world's usurping lord
At a million impious altars
  His own proud image adored,
God spake as He stept from His ambush:
  "O great in thine own conceit,
I will show thee thy source, how humble,
  Thy goal, for a god how unmeet."

Thereat, by the word of the Maker
  The Spirit of Man was led
To a mighty peak of vision,
  Where God to His creature said:
"Look eastward toward time's sunrise."
  And, age upon age untold,
The Spirit of Man saw clearly
  The Past as a chart out-rolled, —
Beheld his base beginnings
  In the depths of time, and his strife
With beasts and crawling horrors
  For leave to live, when life

Meant but to slay and to procreate,
  To feed and to sleep, among
Mere mouths, voracities boundless,
  Blind lusts, desires without tongue,
And ferocities vast, fulfilling
  Their being's malignant law,
While nature was one hunger,
  And one hate, all fangs and maw.

With that, for a single moment,
  Abashed at his own descent,
In humbleness Man's Spirit
  At the feet of the Maker bent ;
But, swifter than light, he recovered
  The stature and pose of his pride,
And, " Think not thus to shame me
  With my mean birth," he cried.
"This is my loftiest greatness,
  To have been born so low ;
Greater than Thou the ungrowing
  Am I that for ever grow."
And God forbore to rebuke him,
  But answered brief and stern,
Bidding him toward time's sunset
  His vision westward turn ;

And the Spirit of Man obeying
  Beheld as a chart out-rolled
The likeness and form of the Future,
  Age upon age untold ;
Beheld his own meridian,
  And beheld his dark decline,
His secular fall to nadir
  From summits of light divine,
Till at last, amid worlds exhausted,
  And bankrupt of force and fire,
'Twas his, in a torrent of darkness,
  Like a sputtering lamp to expire.

Then a war of shame and anger
  Did the realm of his soul divide ;
" 'Tis false, 'tis a lying vision,"
  In the face of his God he cried.
" Thou thinkest to daunt me with shadows ;
  Not such as Thou feign'st is my doom :
From glory to rise unto glory
  Is mine, who have risen from gloom.
I doubt if Thou knew'st at my making
  How near to Thy throne I should climb,
O'er the mountainous slopes of the ages
  And the conquered peaks of time.

Nor shall I look backward nor rest me
    Till the uttermost heights I have trod,
And am equalled with Thee or above Thee,
    The mate or the master of God."

Ev'n thus Man turned from the Maker,
    With thundered defiance wild,
And God with a terrible silence
    Reproved the speech of His child.
And man returned to his labours,
    And stiffened the neck of his will;
And the æons still went rolling,
    And his power was crescent still.
But yet there remained to conquer
    One foe, and the greatest — although
Despoiled of his ancient terrors,
    At heart, as of old, a foe —
Unmaker of all, and renewer,
    Who winnows the world with his wing,
The Lord of Death, the undying,
    Ev'n Asraël the King.

And lo, Man mustered his forces
    The war of wars to wage,
And with storm and thunder of onset
    Did the foe of foes engage,

And the Lord of Death, the undying,
   Was beset and harried sore,
In his immemorial fastness
   At night's aboriginal core.
And during years a thousand
   Man leaguered his enemy's hold,
While nature was one deep tremor,
   And the heart of the world waxed cold,
Till the phantom battlements wavered,
   And the ghostly fortress fell,
And Man with shadowy fetters
   Bound fast great Asraël.

So, to each star in the heavens,
   The exultant word was blown,
The annunciation tremendous,
   Death is overthrown !
And Space in her ultimate borders
   Prolonging the jubilant tone,
With hollow ingeminations,
   Sighed, *Death is overthrown !*
And God in His house of silence,
   Where He dwelleth aloof, alone,
Paused in His tasks to hearken :
   Death is overthrown !

Then a solemn and high thanksgiving
　　By Man unto Man was sung,
In his temples of self-adoration,
　　With his own multitudinous tongue ;
And he said to his Soul : " Rejoice thou,
　　For thy last great foe lies bound,
Ev'n Asraël the Unmaker,
　　Unmade, disarmed, discrowned."

And behold, his Soul rejoiced not,
　　The breath of whose being was strife,
For life with nothing to vanquish
　　Seemed but the shadow of life.
No goal invited and promised
　　And divinely provocative shone ;
And Fear having fled, her sister,
　　Blest Hope, in her train was gone ;
And the coping and crown of achievement
　　Was hell than defeat more dire —
The torment of all-things-compassed,
　　The plague of nought-to-desire ;
And Man the invincible queller,
　　Man with his foot on his foes,
In boundless satiety hungred,
　　Restless from utter repose,

Victor of nature, victor
  Of the prince of the powers of the air,
By mighty weariness vanquished,
  And crowned with august despair.

Then, at his dreadful zenith,
  He cried unto God : " O Thou
Whom of old in my days of striving
  Methought I needed not, — now,
In this my abject glory,
  My hopeless and helpless might,
Hearken and cheer and succour ! "
  And God from His lonely height,
From eternity's passionless summits,
  On suppliant Man looked down,
And His brow waxed human with pity,
  Belying its awful crown.
" Thy richest possession," He answered,
  " Blest Hope, will I restore,
And the infinite wealth of weakness
  Which was thy strength of yore ;
And I will arouse from slumber,
  In his hold where bound he lies,
Thine enemy most benefic ; —
  O Asraël, hear and rise ! "

And a sound like the heart of nature
    Riven and cloven and torn,
Announced, to the ear universal,
    Undying Death new-born.
Sublime he rose in his fetters,
    And shook the chains aside
Ev'n as some mortal sleeper
    'Mid forests in autumntide
Rises and shakes off lightly
    The leaves that lightly fell
On his limbs and his hair unheeded
    While as yet he slumbered well.

And Deity paused and hearkened,
    Then turned to the undivine,
Saying, " O Man, My creature,
    Thy lot was more blest than Mine.
I taste not delight of seeking,
    Nor the boon of longing know.
There is but one joy transcendent,
    And I hoard it not but bestow.
I hoard it not nor have tasted,
    But freely I gave it to thee —
The joy of most glorious striving,
    Which dieth in victory."

Thus, to the Soul of the Dreamer,
   This Dream out of darkness flew,
Through the horn or the ivory portal,
   But he wist not which of the two.

MISCELLANEOUS

PRELUDE

The mighty poets from their flowing store
Dispense like casual alms the careless ore ;
Through throngs of men their lonely way they go,
Let fall their costly thoughts, nor seem to know. —
Not mine the rich and showering hand, that strews
The facile largess of a stintless Muse.
A fitful presence, seldom tarrying long,
Capriciously she touches me to song —
Then leaves me to lament her flight in vain,
And wonder will she ever come again.

67

AUTUMN

Thou burden of all songs the earth hath sung,
    Thou retrospect in Time's reverted eyes,
    Thou metaphor of everything that dies,
That dies ill-starred, or dies beloved and young
        And therefore blest and wise, —
O be less beautiful, or be less brief,
    Thou tragic splendour, strange, and full of fear !
    In vain her pageant shall the Summer rear?
At thy mute signal, leaf by golden leaf,
        Crumbles the gorgeous year.

Ah, ghostly as remembered mirth, the tale
    Of Summer's bloom, the legend of the Spring !
    And thou, too, flutterest an impatient wing,
Thou presence yet more fugitive and frail,
        Thou most unbodied thing,
Whose very being is thy going hence,
    And passage and departure all thy theme ;
    Whose life doth still a splendid dying seem,

And thou at height of thy magnificence
  A figment and a dream.

Stilled is the virgin rapture that was June,
 And cold is August's panting heart of fire ;
 And in the storm-dismantled forest-choir
For thine own elegy thy winds attune
  Their wild and wizard lyre :
And poignant grows the charm of thy decay,
 The pathos of thy beauty, and the sting,
 Thou parable of greatness vanishing !
For me, thy woods of gold and skies of grey
  With speech fantastic ring.

For me, to dreams resigned, there come and go,
 'Twixt mountains draped and hooded night and morn,
 Elusive notes in wandering wafture borne,
From undiscoverable lips that blow
  An immaterial horn ;
And spectral seem thy winter-boding trees,
 Thy ruinous bowers and drifted foliage wet —
 O Past and Future in sad bridal met,
O voice of everything that perishes,
  And soul of all regret !

WORLD-STRANGENESS

STRANGE the world about me lies,
    Never yet familiar grown —
Still disturbs me with surprise,
    Haunts me like a face half known.

In this house with starry dome,
    Floored with gemlike plains and seas,
Shall I never feel at home,
    Never wholly be at ease?

On from room to room I stray,
    Yet my Host can ne'er espy,
And I know not to this day
    Whether guest or captive I.

So, between the starry dome
    And the floor of plains and seas,
I have never felt at home,
    Never wholly been at ease.

"WHEN BIRDS WERE SONGLESS"

When birds were songless on the bough
  I heard thee sing.
The world was full of winter, thou
  Wert full of spring.

To-day the world's heart feels anew
  The vernal thrill,
And thine beneath the rueful yew
  Is wintry chill.

71

THE MOCK SELF

Few friends are mine, though many wights there be
Who, meeting oft a phantasm that makes claim
To be myself, and hath my face and name,
And whose thin fraud I wink at privily,
Account this light impostor very me.
What boots it undeceive them, and proclaim
Myself myself, and whelm this cheat with shame?
I care not, so he leave my true self free,
Impose not on me also; but alas!
I too, at fault, bewildered, sometimes take
Him for myself, and far from mine own sight,
Torpid, indifferent, doth mine own self pass;
And yet anon leaps suddenly awake,
And spurns the gibbering mime into the night.

"THY VOICE FROM INMOST DREAMLAND CALLS"

Thy voice from inmost dreamland calls ;
  The wastes of sleep thou makest fair ;
Bright o'er the ridge of darkness falls
  The cataract of thy hair.

The morn renews its golden birth :
  Thou with the vanquished night dost fade ;
And leav'st the ponderable earth
  Less real than thy shade.

73

THE FLIGHT OF YOUTH

Youth ! ere thou be flown away,
Surely one last boon to-day
    Thou'lt bestow —
One last light of rapture give,
Rich and lordly fugitive !
    Ere thou go.

What, thou canst not?   What, all spent?
All thy spells of ravishment
    Pow'rless now?
Gone thy magic out of date?
Gone, all gone that made thee great? —
    Follow thou !

"NAY, BID ME NOT MY CARES TO LEAVE"

NAY, bid me not my cares to leave,
    Who cannot from their shadow flee.
I do but win a short reprieve,
    'Scaping to pleasure and to thee.

I may, at best, a moment's grace,
    And grant of liberty, obtain ;
Respited for a little space,
    To go back into bonds again.

75

A CHILD'S HAIR

A LETTER from abroad.   I tear
Its sheathing open, unaware
What treasure gleams within ; and there —
    Like bird from cage —
Flutters a curl of golden hair
    Out of the page.

From such a frolic head 'twas shorn !
('Tis but five years since he was born.)
Not sunlight scampering over corn
    Were merrier thing.
A child?   A fragment of the morn,
    A piece of Spring !

Surely an ampler, fuller day
Than drapes our English skies with grey —
A deeper light, a richer ray

Than here we know —
To this bright tress have given away
Their living glow.

For Willie dwells where gentian flowers
Make mimic sky in mountain bowers;
And vineyards steeped in ardent hours
Slope to the wave
Where storied Chillon's tragic towers
Their bases lave;

And over piny tracts of Vaud
The rose of eve steals up the snow;
And on the waters far below
Strange sails like wings
Half-bodilessly come and go,
Fantastic things;

And tender night falls like a sigh
On *châlet* low and *château* high;
And the far cataract's voice comes nigh,
Where no man hears;
And spectral peaks impale the sky
On silver spears.

Ah, Willie, whose dissevered tress
Lies in my hand ! — may you possess
At least one sovereign happiness,
  Ev'n to your grave ;
One boon than which I ask naught less,
  Naught greater crave :

May cloud and mountain, lake and vale,
Never to you be trite or stale
As unto souls whose wellsprings fail
  Or flow defiled,
Till Nature's happiest fairy-tale
  Charms not her child !

For when the spirit waxes numb,
Alien and strange these shows become,
And stricken with life's tedium
  The streams run dry,
The choric spheres themselves are dumb,
  And dead the sky, —

Dead as to captives grown supine,
Chained to their task in sightless mine :
Above, the bland day smiles benign,

Birds carol free,
In thunderous throes of life divine
Leaps the glad sea ;

But they — their day and night are one.
What is't to them, that rivulets run,
Or what concern of theirs the sun?
It seems as though
Their business with these things was done
Ages ago :

Only, at times, each dulled heart feels
That somewhere, sealed with hopeless seals,
The unmeaning heaven about him reels,
And he lies hurled
Beyond the roar of all the wheels
Of all the world.

.   .   .   .   .

On what strange track one's fancies fare !
To eyeless night in sunless lair
'Tis a far cry from Willie's hair ;
And here it lies —
Human, yet something which can ne'er
Grow sad and wise :

Which, when the head where late it lay
In life's grey dusk itself is grey,
And when the curfew of life's day
        By death is tolled,
Shall forfeit not the auroral ray
        And eastern gold.

THE KEY–BOARD

FIVE-AND-THIRTY black slaves,
   Half-a-hundred white,
All their duty but to sing
   For their Queen's delight,
Now with throats of thunder,
   Now with dulcet lips,
While she rules them royally
   With her finger-tips !

When she quits her palace,
   All the slaves are dumb —
Dumb with dolour till the Queen
   Back to Court is come :
Dumb the throats of thunder,
   Dumb the dulcet lips,
Lacking all the sovereignty
   Of her finger-tips.

Dusky slaves and pallid,
　　Ebon slaves and white,
When the Queen was on her throne
　　How you sang to-night !
Ah, the throats of thunder !
　　Ah, the dulcet lips !
Ah, the gracious tyrannies
　　Of her finger-tips !

Silent, silent, silent,
　　All your voices now ;
Was it then her life alone
　　Did your life endow?
Waken, throats of thunder !
　　Waken, dulcet lips !
Touched to immortality
　　By her finger-tips.

"SCENTLESS FLOW'RS I BRING THEE"

SCENTLESS flow'rs I bring thee — yet
In thy bosom be they set ;
In thy bosom each one grows
Fragrant beyond any rose.

Sweet enough were she who could,
In thy heart's sweet neighbourhood,
Some redundant sweetness thus
Borrow from that overplus.

83

ON LANDOR'S "HELLENICS"

Come hither, who grow cloyed to surfeiting
With lyric draughts o'ersweet, from rills that rise
On Hybla not Parnassus mountain : come
With beakers rinsed of the dulcifluous wave
Hither, and see a magic miracle
Of happiest science, the bland Attic skies
True-mirrored by an English well ; — no stream
Whose heaven-belying surface makes the stars
Reel, with its restless idiosyncrasy ;
But well unstirred, save when at times it takes
Tribute of lover's eyelids, and at times
Bubbles with laughter of some sprite below.

84

TO ———

(WITH A VOLUME OF EPIGRAMS)

UNTO the Lady of The Nook
    Fly, tiny book.
There thou hast lovers — even thou !
    Fly thither now.

Seven years hast thou for honour yearned,
    And scant praise earned ;
But ah ! to win, at last, *such* friends,
    Is full amends.

ON EXAGGERATED DEFERENCE TO
FOREIGN LITERARY OPINION

WHAT ! and shall *we*, with such submissive airs
As age demands in reverence from the young,
Await these crumbs of praise from Europe flung,
And doubt of our own greatness till it bears
The signet of your Goethes or Voltaires?
We who alone in latter times have sung
With scarce less power than Arno's exiled tongue —
We who are Milton's kindred, Shakespeare's heirs.
The prize of lyric victory who shall gain
If ours be not the laurel, ours the palm?
More than the froth and flotsam of the Seine,
More than your Hugo-flare against the night,
And more than Weimar's proud elaborate calm,
One flash of Byron's lightning, Wordsworth's light.

ENGLAND TO IRELAND

(FEBRUARY 1888)

SPOUSE whom my sword in the olden time won me,
   Winning me hatred more sharp than a sword —
Mother of children who hiss at or shun me,
   Curse or revile me, and hold me abhorred —
Heiress of anger that nothing assuages,
   Mad for the future, and mad from the past —
Daughter of all the implacable ages,
   Lo, let us turn and be lovers at last !

Lovers whom tragical sin hath made equal,
   One in transgression and one in remorse.
Bonds may be severed, but what were the sequel?
   Hardly shall amity come of divorce.
Let the dead Past have a royal entombing,
   O'er it the Future built white for a fane !
I that am haughty from much overcoming
   Sue to thee, supplicate — nay, is it vain?

Hate and mistrust are the children of blindness, —
　　Could we but see one another, 'twere well !
Knowledge is sympathy, charity, kindness,
　　Ignorance only is maker of hell.
Could we but gaze for an hour, for a minute,
　　Deep in each other's unfaltering eyes,
Love were begun — for that look would begin it —
　　Born in the flash of a mighty surprise.

Then should the ominous night-bird of Error,
　　Scared by a sudden irruption of day,
Flap his maleficent wings, and in terror
　　Flit to the wilderness, dropping his prey.
Then should we, growing in strength and in sweetness,
　　Fusing to one indivisible soul,
Dazzle the world with a splendid completeness,
　　Mightily single, immovably whole.

Thou, like a flame when the stormy winds fan it,
　　I, like a rock to the elements bare, —
Mixed by love's magic, the fire and the granite,
　　Who should compete with us, what should compare ?
Strong with a strength that no fate might dissever,
　　One with a oneness no force could divide,
So were we married and mingled for ever,
　　Lover with lover, and bridegroom with bride.

MENSIS LACRIMARUM

(MARCH 1885)

MARCH, that comes roaring, maned, with rampant paws,
  And bleatingly withdraws ;
March, — 'tis the year's fantastic nondescript,
  That, born when frost hath nipped
The shivering fields, or tempest scarred the hills,
  Dies crowned with daffodils.
The month of the renewal of the earth
  By mingled death and birth :
But, England ! in this latest of thy years
  Call it — the Month of Tears.

"UNDER THE DARK AND PINY STEEP"

Under the dark and piny steep
  We watched the storm crash by :
We saw the bright brand leap and leap
  Out of the shattered sky.

The elements were minist'ring
  To make one mortal blest ;
For, peal by peal, you did but cling
  The closer to his breast.

THE BLIND SUMMIT

[A Viennese gentleman, who had climbed the Hoch-König without a guide, was found dead, in a sitting posture, near the summit, upon which he had written, " It is cold, and clouds shut out the view." — *Vide* the *Daily News* of September 10, 1891.]

So mounts the child of ages of desire,
Man, up the steeps of Thought ; and would behold
Yet purer peaks, touched with unearthlier fire,
In sudden prospect virginally new ;
But on the lone last height he sighs : " 'Tis cold,
And clouds shut out the view."

Ah, doom of mortals ! Vexed with phantoms old,
Old phantoms that waylay us and pursue, —
Weary of dreams, — we think to see unfold
The eternal landscape of the Real and True ;
And on our Pisgah can but write : " 'Tis cold,
And clouds shut out the view."

TO LORD TENNYSON

(With a Volume of Verse)

Master and mage, our prince of song, whom Time,
  In this your autumn mellow and serene,
  Crowns ever with fresh laurels, nor less green
Than garlands dewy from your verdurous prime ;
Heir of the riches of the whole world's rhyme,
  Dow'r'd with the Doric grace, the Mantuan mien,
  With Arno's depth and Avon's golden sheen ;
Singer to whom the singing ages climb,
Convergent ; — if the youngest of the choir
  May snatch a flying splendour from your name
Making his page illustrious, and aspire
  For one rich moment your regard to claim,
Suffer him at your feet to lay his lyre
  And touch the skirts and fringes of your fame.

SKETCH OF A POLITICAL CHARACTER

(1885)

THERE is a race of men, who master life,
Their victory being inversely as their strife ;
Who capture by refraining from pursuit ;
Shake not the bough, yet load their hands with fruit ;
The earth's high places who attain to fill,
By most indomitably sitting still.
While others, full upon the fortress hurled,
Lay fiery siege to the embattled world,
Of such rude arts *their* natures feel no need ;
Greatly inert, they lazily succeed ;
Find in the golden mean their proper bliss,
And doing nothing, never do amiss ;
But lapt in men's good graces live, and die
By all regretted, nobody knows why.

Cast in this fortunate Olympian mould,
The admirable *   *   *   * behold ;

Whom naught could dazzle or mislead, unless
'Twere the wild light of fatal cautiousness ;
Who never takes a step from his own door
But he looks backward ere he looks before.
When once he starts, it were too much to say
He visibly gets farther on his way :
But all allow, he ponders well his course —
For future uses hoarding present force.
The flippant deem him slow and saturnine,
The summed-up phlegm of that illustrious line ;
But we, his honest adversaries, who
More highly prize him than his false friends do,
Frankly admire that simple mass and weight —
A solid Roman pillar of the State,
So inharmonious with the baser style
Of neighbouring columns grafted on the pile,
So proud and imperturbable and chill,
Chosen and matched so excellently ill,
He seems a monument of pensive grace,
Ah, how pathetically out of place !

Would that some call he could not choose but heed —
Of private passion or of public need —
At last might sting to life that slothful power,
And snare him into greatness for an hour !

ART MAXIMS

OFTEN ornateness
Goes with greatness ;
Oftener felicity
Comes of simplicity.

Talent that's cheapest
Affects singularity.
Thoughts that dive deepest
Rise radiant in clarity.

Life is rough :
Sing smoothly, O Bard.
Enough, enough,
To have *found* life hard.

No record Art keeps
Of her travail and throes.
There is toil on the steeps, —
On the summits, repose.

THE GLIMPSE

Just for a day you crossed my life's dull track,
  Put my ignobler dreams to sudden shame,
Went your bright way, and left me to fall back
  On my own world of poorer deed and aim ;

To fall back on my meaner world, and feel
  Like one who, dwelling 'mid some smoke-dimmed
    town, —
In a brief pause of labour's sullen wheel, —
  'Scaped from the street's dead dust and factory's
    frown, —

In stainless daylight saw the pure seas roll,
  Saw mountains pillaring the perfect sky :
Then journeyed home, to carry in his soul
  The torment of the difference till he die.

LINES

(With a Volume of the Author's Poems sent to M. R. C.)

Go, Verse, nor let the grass of tarrying grow
Beneath thy feet iambic.   Southward go
O'er Thamesis his stream, nor halt until
Thou reach the summit of a suburb hill
To lettered fame not unfamiliar : there
Crave rest and shelter of a scholiast fair,
Who dwelleth in a world of old romance,
Magic emprise and faery chevisaunce.
Tell her, that he who made thee, years ago,
By northern stream and mountain, and where blow
Great breaths from the sea-sunset, at this day
One half thy fabric fain would rase away ;
But she must take thee faults and all, my Verse,
Forgive thy better and forget thy worse.
Thee, doubtless, she shall place, not scorned, among
More famous songs by happier minstrels sung ; —
In Shakespeare's shadow thou shalt find a home,
Shalt house with melodists of Greece and Rome,

Or awed by Dante's wintry presence be,
Or won by Goethe's regal suavity,
Or with those masters hardly less adored
Repose, of Rydal and of Farringford ;
And — like a mortal rapt from men's abodes
Into some skyey fastness of the gods —
Divinely neighboured, thou in such a shrine
Mayst for a moment dream thyself divine.

THE RAVEN'S SHADOW

SEABIRD, elemental sprite,
　　Moulded of the sun and spray —
Raven, dreary flake of night
　　Drifting in the eye of day —
What in common have ye two,
Meeting 'twixt the blue and blue?

Thou to eastward carriest
　　The keen savour of the foam, —
Thou dost bear unto the west
　　Fragrance from thy woody home,
Where perchance a house is thine
Odorous of the oozy pine.

Eastward thee thy proper cares,
　　Things of mighty moment, call;
Thee to westward thine affairs
　　Summon, weighty matters all:

I, where land and sea contest,
Watch you eastward, watch you west,

Till, in snares of fancy caught,
    Mystically changed ye seem,
And the bird becomes a thought,
    And the thought becomes a dream,
And the dream, outspread on high,
Lords it o'er the abject sky.

Surely I have known before
    Phantoms of the shapes ye be —
Haunters of another shore
    'Leaguered by another sea.
There my wanderings night and morn
Reconcile me to the bourn.

There the bird of happy wings
    Wafts the ocean-news I crave ;
Rumours of an isle he brings
    Gemlike on the golden wave :
But the baleful beak and plume
Scatter immelodious gloom.

Though the flow'rs be faultless made,
    Perfectly to live and die —

Though the bright clouds bloom and fade
　　Flow'rlike 'midst a meadowy sky —
Where this raven roams forlorn
Veins of midnight flaw the morn.

He not less will croak and croak
　　As he ever caws and caws,
Till the starry dance be broke,
　　Till the sphery pæan pause,
And the universal chime
Falter out of tune and time.

Coils the labyrinthine sea
　　Duteous to the lunar will,
But some discord stealthily
　　Vexes the world-ditty still,
And the bird that caws and caws
Clasps creation with his claws.

LUX PERDITA

THINE were the weak, slight hands
That might have taken this strong soul, and bent
Its stubborn substance to thy soft intent,
And bound it unresisting, with such bands
As not the arm of envious heaven had rent.

Thine were the calming eyes
That round my pinnace could have stilled the sea,
And drawn thy voyager home, and bid him be
Pure with their pureness, with their wisdom wise,
Merged in their light, and greatly lost in thee.

But thou — thou passed'st on,
With whiteness clothed of dedicated days,
Cold, like a star ; and me in alien ways
Thou leftest following life's chance lure, where shone
The wandering gleam that beckons and betrays.

HISTORY

HERE, peradventure, in this mirror glassed,
Who gazes long and well at times beholds
Some sunken feature of the mummied Past,
But oftener only the embroidered folds
And soiled magnificence of her rent robe
Whose tattered skirts are ruined dynasties
That sweep the dust of æons in our eyes
And with their trailing pride cumber the globe. —
For lo ! the high, imperial Past is dead :
The air is full of its dissolvèd bones ;
Invincible armies long since vanquishèd,
Kings that remember not their awful thrones,
Powerless potentates and foolish sages,
Impede the slow steps of the pompous ages.

IRELAND

(DECEMBER 1, 1890)

IN the wild and lurid desert, in the thunder-travelled
  ways,
'Neath the night that ever hurries to the dawn that
  still delays,
There she clutches at illusions, and she seeks a
  phantom goal
With the unattaining passion that consumes the un-
  sleeping soul :
And calamity enfolds her, like the shadow of a ban,
And the niggardness of Nature makes the misery of
  man :
And in vain the hand is stretched to lift her, stum-
  bling in the gloom,
While she follows the mad fen-fire that conducts her
  to her doom.

THE LUTE-PLAYER

She was a lady great and splendid,
    I was a minstrel in her halls.
A warrior like a prince attended
    Stayed his steed by the castle walls.

Far had he fared to gaze upon her.
    "O rest thee now, Sir Knight," she said.
The warrior wooed, the warrior won her,
    In time of snowdrops they were wed.
I made sweet music in his honour,
    And longed to strike him dead.

I passed at midnight from her portal,
    Throughout the world till death I rove:
Ah, let me make this lute immortal
    With rapture of my hate and love!

"AND THESE — ARE THESE INDEED THE END"

AND these — are these indeed the end,
  This grinning skull, this heavy loam?
Do all green ways whereby we wend
  Lead but to yon ignoble home?

Ah well! Thine eyes invite to bliss;
  Thy lips are hives of summer still.
I ask not other worlds while this
  Proffers me all the sweets I will.

106

THE RUSS AT KARA

O KING of kings, that watching from Thy throne
　　Sufferest the monster of Ust-Kara's hold,
　　With bosom than Siberia's wastes more cold,
And hear'st the wail of captives crushed and prone,
And sett'st no sign in heaven !   Shall naught atone
　　For their wild pangs whose tale is yet scarce told,
　　Women by uttermost woe made deadly bold,
In the far dungeon's night that hid their moan?
Why waits Thy shattering arm, nor smites this Power
　　Whose beak and talons rend the unshielded breast,
　　　Whose wings shed terror and a plague of gloom,
　　Whose ravin is the hearts of the oppressed ;
Whose brood are hell-births — Hate that bides its hour,
　　　Wrath, and a people's curse that loathe their
　　　　doom?

LIBERTY REJECTED

ABOUT this heart thou hast
  Thy chains made fast,
And think'st thou I would be
  Therefrom set free,
And forth unbound be cast?

The ocean would as soon
  Entreat the moon
Unsay the magic verse
  That seals him hers
From silver noon to noon.

She stooped her pearly head
  Seaward, and said :
" Would'st thou I gave to thee
  Thy liberty,
In Time's youth forfeited ? "

And from his inmost hold
   The answer rolled :
" Thy bondman to remain
   Is sweeter pain,
Dearer an hundredfold."

LIFE WITHOUT HEALTH

BEHOLD life builded as a goodly house
And grown a mansion ruinous
With winter blowing through its crumbling walls !
The master paceth up and down his halls,
And in the empty hours
Can hear the tottering of his towers
And tremor of their bases underground.
And oft he starts and looks around
At creaking of a distant door
Or echo of his footfall on the floor,
Thinking it may be one whom he awaits
And hath for many days awaited,
Coming to lead him through the mouldering gates
Out somewhere, from his home dilapidated.

TO A FRIEND

CHAFING AT ENFORCED IDLENESS FROM INTERRUPTED HEALTH

Soon may the edict lapse, that on you lays
This dire compulsion of infertile days,
This hardest penal toil, reluctant rest !
Meanwhile I count you eminently blest,
Happy from labours heretofore well done,
Happy in tasks auspiciously begun.
For they are blest that have not much to rue —
That have not oft mis-heard the prompter's cue,
Stammered and stumbled and the wrong parts played,
And life a Tragedy of Errors made.

111

"WELL HE SLUMBERS, GREATLY SLAIN"

WELL he slumbers, greatly slain,
  Who in splendid battle dies;
Deep his sleep in midmost main
  Pillowed upon pearl who lies.

Ease, of all good gifts the best,
  War and wave at last decree:
Love alone denies us rest,
  Crueller than sword or sea.

AN EPISTLE

(To N. A.)

So, into Cornwall you go down,
And leave me loitering here in town.
For me, the ebb of London's wave,
Not ocean-thunder in Cornish cave.
My friends (save only one or two)
Gone to the glistening marge, like you, —
The opera season with blare and din
Dying sublime in *Lohengrin*, —
Houses darkened, whose blinded panes
All thoughts, save of the dead, preclude, —
The parks a puddle of tropic rains, —
Clubland a pensive solitude, —
For me, now you and yours are flown,
The fellowship of books alone !

For you, the snaky wave, upflung
With writhing head and hissing tongue ;

The weed whose tangled fibres tell
Of some inviolate deep-sea dell;
The faultless, secret-chambered shell,
Whose sound is an epitome
Of all the utterance of the sea;
Great, basking, twinkling wastes of brine;
Far clouds of gulls that wheel and swerve
In unanimity divine,
With undulation serpentine,
And wondrous, consentaneous curve,
Flashing in sudden silver sheen,
Then melting on the sky-line keen;
The world-forgotten coves that seem
Lapt in some magic old sea-dream,
Where, shivering off the milk-white foam,
Lost airs wander, seeking home,
And into clefts and caverns peep,
Fissures paven with powdered shell,
Recesses of primeval sleep,
Tranced with an immemorial spell;
The granite fangs eternally
Rending the blanch'd lips of the sea;
The breaker clutching land, then hurled
Back on its own tormented world;
The mountainous upthunderings,
The glorious energy of things,

The power, the joy, the cosmic thrill,
Earth's ecstasy made visible,
World-rapture old as Night and new
As sunrise; — this, all this, for you!

So, by Atlantic breezes fanned,
You roam the limits of the land,
And I in London's world abide,
Poor flotsam on the human tide! —
Nay, rather, isled amid the stream —
Watching the flood — and, half in dream
Guessing the sources whence it rose,
And musing to what Deep it flows.

For still the ancient riddles mar
Our joy in man, in leaf, in star.
The Whence and Whither give no rest,
The Wherefore is a hopeless quest;
And the dull wight who never thinks, —
Who, chancing on the sleeping Sphinx,
Passes unchallenged, — fares the best!

But ill it suits this random verse
The high enigmas to rehearse,
And touch with desultory tongue
Secrets no man from Night hath wrung.

We ponder, question, doubt — and pray
The Deep to answer Yea or Nay;
And what does the engirdling wave,
The undivulging, yield us, save
Aspersion of bewildering spray?
We do but dally on the beach,
Writing our little thoughts full large,
While Ocean with imperious speech
Derides us trifling by the marge.
Nay, we are children, who all day
Beside the unknown waters play,
And dig with small toy-spade the sand,
Thinking our trenches wondrous deep,
Till twilight falls, and hand-in-hand
Nurse takes us home, well tired, to sleep;
Sleep, and forget our toys, and be
Lulled by the great unsleeping sea.

Enough ! — to Cornwall you go down,
And I tag rhymes in London town.

TO AUSTIN DOBSON

Yes ! urban is your Muse, and owns
An empire based on London stones;
Yet flow'rs, as mountain violets sweet,
Spring from the pavement 'neath her feet.

Of wilder birth this Muse of mine,
Hill-cradled, and baptized with brine ;
And 'tis for her a sweet despair
To watch that courtly step and air !

Yet surely she, without reproof,
Greeting may send from realms aloof,
And even claim a tie in blood,
And dare to deem it sisterhood.

For well we know, those Maidens be
All daughters of Mnemosyne ;
And 'neath the unifying sun,
Many the songs — but Song is one.

TO EDWARD CLODD

FRIEND, in whose friendship I am twice well-starred,
   A debt not time may cancel is your due ;
   For was it not your praise that earliest drew,
On me obscure, that chivalrous regard,
Ev'n his, who, knowing fame's first steep how hard,
   With generous lips no faltering clarion blew,
   Bidding men hearken to a lyre by few
Heeded, nor grudge the bay to one more bard?
Bitter the task, year by inglorious year,
Of suitor at the world's reluctant ear.
   One cannot sing for ever, like a bird,
For sole delight of singing !   Him his mate
Suffices, listening with a heart elate ;
   Nor more his joy, if all the rapt heav'n heard.

TO EDWARD DOWDEN

ON RECEIVING FROM HIM A COPY OF "THE LIFE OF SHELLEY"

FIRST, ere I slake my hunger, let me thank
The giver of the feast.   For feast it is,
Though of ethereal, translunary fare —
His story who pre-eminently of men
Seemed nourished upon starbeams and the stuff
Of rainbows, and the tempest, and the foam ;
Who hardly brooked on his impatient soul
The fleshly trammels ; whom at last the sea
Gave to the fire, from whose wild arms the winds
Took him, and shook him broadcast to the world.
In my young days of fervid poesy
He drew me to him with his strange far light, —
He held me in a world all clouds and gleams,
And vasty phantoms, where ev'n Man himself
Moved like a phantom 'mid the clouds and gleams.
Anon the Earth recalled me, and a voice
Murmuring of dethroned divinities

And dead times deathless upon sculptured urn —
And Philomela's long-descended pain
Flooding the night — and maidens of romance
To whom asleep St. Agnes' love-dreams come —
Awhile constrained me to a sweet duresse
And thraldom, lapping me in high content,
Soft as the bondage of white amorous arms.
And then a third voice, long unheeded — held
Claustral and cold, and dissonant and tame —
Found me at last with ears to hear.   It sang
Of lowly sorrows and familiar joys,
Of simple manhood, artless womanhood,
And childhood fragrant as the limpid morn ;
And from the homely matter nigh at hand
Ascending and dilating, it disclosed
Spaces and avenues, calm heights and breadths
Of vision, whence I saw each blade of grass
With roots that groped about eternity,
And in each drop of dew upon each blade
The mirror of the inseparable All.
The first voice, then the second, in their turns
Had sung me captive.   This voice sang me free.
Therefore, above all vocal sons of men,
Since him whose sightless eyes saw hell and heaven,
To Wordsworth be my homage, thanks, and love.
Yet dear is Keats, a lucid presence, great

With somewhat of a glorious soullessness.
And dear, and great with an excess of soul,
Shelley, the hectic flamelike rose of verse,
All colour, and all odour, and all bloom,
Steeped in the noonlight, glutted with the sun,
But somewhat lacking root in homely earth,
Lacking such human moisture as bedews
His not less starward stem of song, who, rapt
Not less in glowing vision, yet retained
His clasp of the prehensible, retained
The warm touch of the world that lies to hand,
Not in vague dreams of man forgetting men,
Nor in vast morrows losing the to-day;
Who trusted nature, trusted fate, nor found
An Ogre, sovereign on the throne of things;
Who felt the incumbence of the unknown, yet bore
Without resentment the Divine reserve;
Who suffered not his spirit to dash itself
Against the crags and wavelike break in spray,
But 'midst the infinite tranquillities
Moved tranquil, and henceforth, by Rotha stream
And Rydal's mountain-mirror, and where flows
Yarrow thrice sung or Duddon to the sea,
And wheresoe'er man's heart is thrilled by tones
Struck from man's lyric heartstrings, shall survive.

FELICITY

A SQUALID, hideous town, where streams run black
With vomit of a hundred roaring mills, —
Hither occasion calls me ; and ev'n here,
All in the sable reek that wantonly
Defames the sunlight and deflowers the morn,
One may at least surmise the sky still blue.
Ev'n here, the myriad slaves of the machine
Deem life a boon ; and here, in days far sped,
I overheard a kind-eyed girl relate
To her companions, how a favouring chance
By some few shillings weekly had increased
The earnings of her household, and she said :
" So now we are happy, having all we wished," —
Felicity indeed ! though more it lay
In wanting little than in winning all.

Felicity indeed !   Across the years
To me her tones come back, rebuking ; me,
Spreader of toils to snare the wandering Joy

No guile may capture and no force surprise —
Only by them that never wooed her, won.

O curst with wide desires and spacious dreams,
Too cunningly do ye accumulate
Appliances and means of happiness,
E'er to be happy ! Lavish hosts, ye make
Elaborate preparation to receive
A shy and simple guest, who, warned of all
The ceremony and circumstance wherewith
Ye mean to entertain her, will not come.

A GOLDEN HOUR

A BECKONING spirit of gladness seemed afloat,
   That lightly danced in laughing air before us :
The earth was all in tune, and you a note
     Of Nature's happy chorus.

'Twas like a vernal morn, yet overhead
   The leafless boughs across the lane were knitting :
The ghost of some forgotten Spring, we said,
     O'er Winter's world comes flitting.

Or was it Spring herself, that, gone astray,
   Beyond the alien frontier chose to tarry?
Or but some bold outrider of the May,
     Some April-emissary?

The apparition faded on the air,
   Capricious and incalculable comer. —
Wilt thou too pass, and leave my chill days bare,
     And fall'n my phantom Summer?

AT THE GRAVE OF CHARLES LAMB,
IN EDMONTON

NOT here, O teeming City, was it meet
 Thy lover, thy most faithful, should repose,
 But where the multitudinous life-tide flows
Whose ocean-murmur was to him more sweet
Than melody of birds at morn, or bleat
 Of flocks in Spring-time, *there* should Earth enclose
 His earth, amid thy thronging joys and woes,
There, 'neath the music of thy million feet.
In love of thee this lover knew no peer.
 Thine eastern or thy western fane had made
 Fit habitation for his noble shade.
Mother of mightier, nurse of none more dear,
Not here, in rustic exile, O not here,
 Thy Elia like an alien should be laid !

LINES IN A FLYLEAF OF "CHRISTABEL"

Inhospitably hast thou entertained,
O Poet, us the bidden to thy board,
Whom in mid-feast, and while our thousand mouths
Are one laudation of the festal cheer,
Thou from thy table dost dismiss, unfilled.
Yet loudlier thee than many a lavish host
We praise, and oftener thy repast half-served
Than many a stintless banquet, prodigally
Through satiate hours prolonged ; nor praise less well
Because with tongues thou hast not cloyed, and lips
That mourn the parsimony of affluent souls,
And mix the lamentation with the laud.

RELUCTANT SUMMER

Reluctant Summer! once, a maid
    Full easy of access,
In many a bee-frequented shade
    Thou didst thy lover bless.
Divinely unreproved I played,
    Then, with each liberal tress—
And art thou grown at last afraid
    Of some too close caress?

Or deem'st that if thou shouldst abide
    My passion might decay?
Thou leav'st me pining and denied,
    Coyly thou say'st me nay.
Ev'n as I woo thee to my side,
    Thou, importuned to stay,
Like Orpheus' half-recovered bride
    Ebb'st from my arms away.

THE GREAT MISGIVING

" Not ours," say some, " the thought of death to dread ;
   Asking no heaven, we fear no fabled hell :
Life is a feast, and we have banqueted —
   Shall not the worms as well ?

" The after-silence, when the feast is o'er,
   And void the places where the minstrels stood,
Differs in nought from what hath been before,
   And is nor ill nor good."

Ah, but the Apparition — the dumb sign —
   The beckoning finger bidding me forego
The fellowship, the converse, and the wine,
   The songs, the festal glow !

And ah, to know not, while with friends I sit,
   And while the purple joy is passed about,
Whether 'tis ampler day divinelier lit
   Or homeless night without ;

And whether, stepping forth, my soul shall see
    New prospects, or fall sheer — a blinded thing !
There is, O grave, thy hourly victory,
    And there, O death, thy sting.

"THE THINGS THAT ARE MORE EXCELLENT"

As we wax older on this earth,
  Till many a toy that charmed us seems
Emptied of beauty, stripped of worth,
  And mean as dust and dead as dreams, —
For gauds that perished, shows that passed,
  Some recompense the Fates have sent:
Thrice lovelier shine the things that last,
  The things that are more excellent.

Tired of the Senate's barren brawl,
  An hour with silence we prefer,
Where statelier rise the woods than all
  Yon towers of talk at Westminster.
Let this man prate and that man plot,
  On fame or place or title bent:
The votes of veering crowds are not
  The things that are more excellent.

Shall we perturb and vex our soul
   For " wrongs " which no true freedom mar,
Which no man's upright walk control,
   And from no guiltless deed debar?
What odds though tonguesters heal, or leave
   Unhealed, the grievance they invent?
To things, not phantoms, let us cleave —
   The things that are more excellent.

Nought nobler is, than to be free :
   The stars of heaven are free because
In amplitude of liberty
   Their joy is to obey the laws.
From servitude to freedom's *name*
   Free thou thy mind in bondage pent ;
Depose the fetich, and proclaim
   The things that are more excellent.

And in appropriate dust be hurled
   That dull, punctilious god, whom they
That call their tiny clan the world,
   Serve and obsequiously obey :
Who con their ritual of Routine,
   With minds to one dead likeness blent,
And never ev'n in dreams have seen
   The things that are more excellent.

To dress, to call, to dine, to break
    No canon of the social code,
The little laws that lacqueys make,
    The futile decalogue of Mode, —
How many a soul for these things lives,
    With pious passion, grave intent !
While Nature careless-handed gives
    The things that are more excellent.

To hug the wealth ye cannot use,
    And lack the riches all may gain, —
O blind and wanting wit to choose,
    Who house the chaff and burn the grain !
And still doth life with starry towers
    Lure to the bright, divine ascent ! —
Be yours the things ye would : be ours
    The things that are more excellent.

The grace of friendship — mind and heart
    Linked with their fellow heart and mind ;
The gains of science, gifts of art ;
    The sense of oneness with our kind ;
The thirst to know and understand —
    A large and liberal discontent :
These are the goods in life's rich hand,
    The things that are more excellent.

In faultless rhythm the ocean rolls,
   A rapturous silence thrills the skies ;
And on this earth are lovely souls,
   That softly look with aidful eyes.
Though dark, O God, Thy course and track,
   I think Thou must at least have meant
That nought which lives should wholly lack
   The things that are more excellent.

BEAUTY'S METEMPSYCHOSIS

THAT beauty such as thine
        Can die indeed,
Were ordinance too wantonly malign :
No wit may reconcile so cold a creed
        With beauty such as thine.

From wave and star and flower
        Some effluence rare
Was lent thee, a divine but transient dower :
Thou yield'st it back from eyes and lips and hair
        To wave and star and flower.

Shouldst thou to-morrow die,
        Thou still shalt be
Found in the rose and met in all the sky :
And from the ocean's heart shalt sing to me,
        Shouldst thou to-morrow die.

ENGLAND MY MOTHER

I

ENGLAND my mother,
Wardress of waters,
Builder of peoples,
   Maker of men, —

Hast thou yet leisure
Left for the muses?
Heed'st thou the songsmith
   Forging the rhyme?

Deafened with tumults,
How canst thou hearken?
Strident is faction,
   Demos is loud.

Lazarus, hungry,
Menaces Dives;
Labour the giant
   Chafes in his hold.

Yet do the songsmiths
Quit not their forges ;
Still on life's anvil
   Forge they the rhyme.

Still the rapt faces
Glow from the furnace :
Breath of the smithy
   Scorches their brows.

Yea, and thou hear'st them ?
So shall the hammers
Fashion not vainly
   Verses of gold.

II

Lo, with the ancient
Roots of man's nature,
Twines the eternal
   Passion of song.

Ever Love fans it,
Ever Life feeds it,
Time cannot age it ;
   Death cannot slay.

Deep in the world-heart
Stand its foundations,
Tangled with all things,
   Twin-made with all.

Nay, what is Nature's
Self, but an endless
Strife toward music,
   Euphony, rhyme?

Trees in their blooming,
Tides in their flowing,
Stars in their circling,
   Tremble with song.

God on His throne is
Eldest of poets :
Unto His measures
   Moveth the Whole.

III

Therefore deride not
Speech of the muses,
England my mother,
   Maker of men.

Nations are mortal,
Fragile is greatness ;
Fortune may fly thee,
    Song shall not fly.

Song the all-girdling,
Song cannot perish :
Men shall make music,
    Man shall give ear.

Not while the choric
Chant of creation
Floweth from all things,
    Poured without pause,

Cease we to echo
Faintly the descant
Whereto for ever
    Dances the world.

IV

So let the songsmith
Proffer his rhyme-gift,
England my mother,
    Maker of men.

Gray grows thy count'nance,
Full of the ages;
Time on thy forehead
  Sits like a dream:

Song is the potion
All things renewing,
Youth's one elixir,
  Fountain of morn.

Thou, at the world-loom
Weaving thy future,
Fitly may'st temper
  Toil with delight.

Deemest thou, labour
Only is earnest?
Grave is all beauty,
  Solemn is joy.

Song is no bauble —
Slight not the songsmith,
England my mother,
  Maker of men.

NIGHT

In the night, in the night,
When thou liest alone,
Ah, the sounds that are blown
   In the freaks of the breeze,
By the spirit that sends
The voice of far friends
   With the sigh of the seas
     In the night!

In the night, in the night,
When thou liest alone,
Ah, the ghosts that make moan
   From the days that are sped:
The old dreams, the old deeds,
The old wound that still bleeds,
   And the face of the dead
     In the night!

In the night, in the night,
When thou liest alone,
With the grass and the stone
   O'er thy chamber so deep,
Ah, the silence at last,
Life's dissonance past,
  And only pure sleep
    In the night !

THE FUGITIVE IDEAL

As some most pure and noble face,
　　Seen in the thronged and hurrying street,
Sheds o'er the world a sudden grace,
　　　　A flying odour sweet,
Then, passing, leaves the cheated sense
Baulked with a phantom excellence ;

So, on our soul the visions rise
　　Of that fair life we never led :
They flash a splendour past our eyes,
　　　　We start, and they are fled :
They pass, and leave us with blank gaze,
Resigned to our ignoble days.

"THE FORESTERS"

(Lines written on the appearance of Lord Tennyson's drama.)

CLEAR as of old the great voice rings to-day,
While Sherwood's oak-leaves twine with Aldworth's
    bay :
The voice of him the master and the sire
Of one whole age and legion of the lyre,
Who sang his morning-song when Coleridge still
Uttered dark oracles from Highgate Hill,
And with new-launchèd argosies of rhyme
Gilds and makes brave this sombreing tide of time.
Far be the hour when lesser brows shall wear
The laurel glorious from that wintry hair —
When he, the sovereign of our lyric day,
In Charon's shallop must be rowed away,
And hear, scarce heeding, 'mid the plash of oar,
The *ave atque vale* from the shore !

To him nor tender nor heroic muse
Did her divine confederacy refuse :

To all its moods the lyre of life he strung,
And notes of death fell deathless from his tongue.
Himself the Merlin of his magic strain,
He bade old glories break in gloom again ;
And so exempted from oblivious doom,
Through him these days shall fadeless break in bloom.

SONG

Lightly we met in the morn,
  Lightly we parted at eve.
There was never a thought of the thorn
  The rose of a day might leave.

Fate's finger we did not perceive,
  So lightly we met in the morn !
So lightly we parted at eve
  We knew not that Love was born.

I rose on the morrow forlorn,
  To pine and remember and grieve.
Too lightly we met in the morn !
  Too lightly we parted at eve !

COLUMBUS

(12TH OCTOBER 1492)

FROM his adventurous prime
He dreamed the dream sublime :
  Over his wandering youth
    It hung, a beckoning star.
At last the vision fled,
And left him in its stead
  The scarce sublimer truth,
    The world he found afar.

The scattered isles that stand
Warding the mightier land
  Yielded their maidenhood
    To his imperious prow.
The mainland within call
Lay vast and virginal :
  In its blue porch he stood :
    No more did fate allow.

No more ! but ah, how much,
To be the first to touch
  The veriest azure hem
    Of that majestic robe !
Lord of the lordly sea,
Earth's mightiest sailor he :
  Great Captain among them,
    The captors of the globe.

When shall the world forget
Thy glory and our debt,
  Indomitable soul,
    Immortal Genoese ?
Not while the shrewd salt gale
Whines amid shroud and sail,
  Above the rhythmic roll
    And thunder of the seas.

SONNETS

FROM

VER TENEBROSUM

A SERIES OF POEMS ON PUBLIC AFFAIRS WRITTEN IN
MARCH AND APRIL 1885

I

The Soudanese

They wrong'd not us, nor sought 'gainst us to wage
The bitter battle.   On their God they cried
For succour, deeming justice to abide
In heaven, if banish'd from earth's vicinage.
And when they rose with a gall'd lion's rage,
We, on the captor's, keeper's, tamer's side,
We, with the alien tyranny allied,
We bade them back to their Egyptian cage.
Scarce knew they who we were !   A wind of blight
From the mysterious far north-west we came.
Our greatness now their veriest babes have learn'd,
Where, in wild desert homes, by day, by night,
Thousands that weep their warriors unreturn'd,
O England, O my country, curse thy name !

II

THE ENGLISH DEAD

GIVE honour to our heroes fall'n, how ill
Soe'er the cause that bade them forth to die.
Honour to him, the untimely struck, whom high
In place, more high in hope, 'twas fate's harsh will
With tedious pain unsplendidly to kill.
Honour to him, doom'd splendidly to die,
Child of the city whose foster-child am I,
Who, hotly leading up the ensanguin'd hill
His charging thousand, fell without a word —
Fell, but shall fall not from our memory.
Also for them let honour's voice be heard
Who nameless sleep, while dull time covereth
With no illustrious shade of laurel tree,
But with the poppy alone, their deeds and death.

III

GORDON

IDLE although our homage be and vain,
Who loudly through the door of silence press
And vie in zeal to crown death's nakedness,
Not therefore shall melodious lips refrain
Thy praises, gentlest warrior without stain,
Denied the happy garland of success,
Foil'd by dark fate, but glorious none the less,
Greatest of losers, on the lone peak slain
Of Alp-like virtue.   Not to-day, and not
To-morrow, shall thy spirit's splendour be
Oblivion's victim ; but when God shall find
All human grandeur among men forgot,
Then only shall the world, grown old and blind,
Cease, in her dotage, to remember Thee.

IV

GORDON (*concluded*)

ARAB, Egyptian, English — by the sword
Cloven, or pierced with spears, or bullet-mown —
In equal fate they sleep : their dust is grown
A portion of the fiery sands abhorred.
And thou, what hast thou, hero, for reward,
Thou, England's glory and her shame?   O'erthrown
Thou liest, unburied, or with grave unknown
As his to whom on Nebo's height the Lord
Showed all the land of Gilead, unto Dan ;
Judah sea-fringed ; Manasseh and Ephraim ;
And Jericho palmy, to where Zoar lay ;
And in a valley of Moab buried him,
Over against Beth-Peor, but no man
Knows of his sepulchre unto this day.

V

Foreign Menace

I marvel that this land, whereof I claim
The glory of sonship — for it *was* erewhile
A glory to be sprung of Britain's isle,
Though now it well-nigh more resembles shame –
I marvel that this land with heart so tame
Can brook the northern insolence and guile.
But most it angers me, to think how vile
Art thou, how base, from whom the insult came,
Unwieldy laggard, many an age behind
Thy sister Powers, in brain and conscience both ;
In recognition of man's widening mind
And flexile adaptation to its growth :
Brute bulk, that bearest on thy back, half loth,
One wretched man, most pitied of mankind.

VI

Home-rootedness

I cannot boast myself cosmopolite ;
I own to " insularity," although
'Tis fall'n from fashion, as full well I know.
For somehow, being a plain and simple wight,
I am skin-deep a child of the new light,
But chiefly am mere Englishman below,
Of island-fostering ; and can hate a foe,
And trust my kin before the Muscovite.
Whom shall I trust if not my kin?   And whom
Account so near in natural bonds as these
Born of my mother England's mighty womb,
Nursed on my mother England's mighty knees,
And lull'd as I was lull'd in glory and gloom
With cradle-song of her protecting seas?

VII

Our Eastern Treasure

In cobwebb'd corners dusty and dim I hear
A thin voice pipingly revived of late,
Which saith our India is a cumbrous weight,
An idle decoration, bought too dear.
The wiser world contemns not gorgeous gear;
Just pride is no mean factor in a State;
The sense of greatness keeps a nation great;
And mighty they who mighty can appear.
It may be that if hands of greed could steal
From England's grasp the envied orient prize,
This tide of gold would flood her still as now:
But were she the same England, made to feel
A brightness gone from out those starry eyes,
A splendour from that constellated brow?

VIII

Nightmare

(*Written during apparent imminence of war*)

In a false dream I saw the Foe prevail.
The war was ended ; the last smoke had rolled
Away : and we, erewhile the strong and bold,
Stood broken, humbled, withered, weak and pale,
And moan'd, " Our greatness is become a tale
To tell our children's babes when we are old.
They shall put by their playthings to be told
How England once, before the years of bale,
Throned above trembling, puissant, grandiose, calm,
Held Asia's richest jewel in her palm ;
And with unnumbered isles barbaric, she
The broad hem of her glistering robe impearl'd ;
Then, when she wound her arms about the world,
And had for vassal the obsequious sea."

THE PRINCE'S QUEST

This Poem, a juvenile production, was first published in 1880.

THE PRINCE'S QUEST

PART THE FIRST

THERE was a time, it passeth me to say
How long ago, but sure 'twas many a day
Before the world had gotten her such store
Of foolish wisdom as she hath, — before
She fell to waxing gray with weight of years
And knowledge, bitter knowledge, bought with tears, —
When it did seem as if the feet of time
Moved to the music of a golden rhyme,
And never one false thread might woven be
Athwart that web of worldwide melody.
'Twas then there lived a certain queen and king,
Unvext of wars or other evil thing,
Within a spacious palace builded high,
Whence they might see their chiefest city lie
About them, and half hear from their tall towers
Its populous murmur through the daylight hours,
And see beyond its walls the pleasant plain.
One child they had, these blissful royal twain :

161

Of whom 'tis told — so more than fair was he —
There lurked at whiles a something shadowy
Deep down within the fairness of his face ;
As 'twere a hint of some not-earthly grace,
Making the royal stripling rather seem
The very dreaming offspring of a dream
Than human child of human ancestry :
And something strange-fantastical was he,
I doubt not.   Howsoever he upgrew,
And after certain years to manhood drew
Nigh, so that all about his father's court,
Seeing his graciousness of princely port,
Rejoiced thereat ; and many maidens' eyes
Look'd pleased upon his beauty, and the sighs
Of many told I know not what sweet tales.

So, like to some fair ship with sunlit sails,
Glided his youth amid a stormless sea,
Till once by night there came mysteriously
A fateful wind, and o'er an unknown deep
Bore him perforce.   It chanced that while in sleep
He lay, there came to him a strange dim dream.
'Twas like as he did float adown a stream,
In a lone boat that had nor sail nor oar
Yet seemed as it would glide for evermore,
Deep in the bosom of a sultry land

Fair with all fairness.   Upon either hand
Were hills green-browed and mist-engarlanded,
And all about their feet were woods bespread,
Hoarding the cool and leafy silentness
In many an unsunned hollow and hid recess.
Nought of unbeauteous might be there espied ;
But in the heart of the deep woods and wide,
And in the heart of all, was Mystery —
A something more than outer eye might see,
A something more than ever ear might hear.
The very birds that came and sang anear
Did seem to syllable some faery tongue,
And, singing much, to hold yet more unsung.
And heard at whiles, with hollow wandering tone,
Far off, as by some aery huntsmen blown,
Faint-echoing horns, among the mountains wound,
Made all the live air tremulous with sound.

So hour by hour (thus ran the Prince's dream)
Glided the boat along the broadening stream ;
Till, being widowed of the sun her lord,
The purblind day went groping evenward :
Whereafter Sleep compelled to his mild yoke
The bubbling clear souls of the feathered folk,
Sealing the vital fountains of their song.
Howbeit the Prince went onward all night long

And never shade of languor came on him,
Nor any weariness his eyes made dim.
And so in season due he heard the breath
Of the brief winds that wake ere darkness' death
Sigh through the woods and all the valley wide :
The rushes by the water answering sighed :
Sighed all the river from its reedy throat.
And like a wingèd creature went the boat,
Over the errant water wandering free,
As some lone seabird over a lone sea.

And Morn pale-haired with watery wide eyes
Look'd up.   And starting with a swift surprise,
Sprang to his feet the Prince, and forward leant,
His gaze on something right before him bent
That like a towered and templed city showed,
Afar off, dim with very light, and glowed
As burnished seas at sundawn when the waves
Make amber lightnings all in dim-roof'd caves
That fling mock-thunder back.   Long leagues away,
Down by the river's green right bank it lay,
Set like a jewel in the golden morn :
But ever as the Prince was onward borne,
Nearer and nearer danced the dizzy fires
Of domes innumerable and sun-tipt spires
And many a sky-acquainted pinnacle,

Splendid beyond what mortal tongue may tell;
And ere the middle heat of day was spent,
He saw, by nearness thrice-magnificent,
Hardly a furlong's space before him lie
The City, sloping to the stream thereby.

And therewithal the boat of its own will
Close to the shore began to glide, until,
All of a sudden passing nigh to where
The glistering white feet of a marble stair
Ran to the rippled brink, the Prince outsprang
Upon the gleamy steps, and wellnigh sang
For joy, to be once more upon his feet,
Amid the green grass and the flowers sweet.
So on he paced along the river-marge,
And saw full many a fair and stately barge,
Adorned with strange device and imagery,
At anchor in the quiet waters lie.
And presently he came unto a gate
Of massy gold, that shone with splendid state
Of mystic hieroglyphs, and storied frieze
All overwrought with carven phantasies.
And in the shadow of the golden gate,
One in the habit of a porter sate,
And on the Prince with wondering eye looked he,
And greeted him with reverent courtesy,

Saying, " Fair sir, thou art of mortal race,
The first hath ever journeyed to this place, —
For well I know thou art a stranger here,
As by the garb thou wearest doth appear ;
And if thy raiment do belie thee not,
Thou should'st be some king's son.   And well I wot,
If that be true was prophesied of yore,
A wondrous fortune is for thee in store ;
For though I be not read in Doomful Writ,
Oft have I heard the wise expounding it,
And, of a truth, the fatal rolls declare
That the first mortal who shall hither fare
Shall surely have our Maiden-Queen to wife,
And while the world lives shall they twain have life."

Hereat, be sure, the wonder-stricken youth,
Holden in doubt if this were lies or truth,
Was tongue-tied with amaze, and sore perplext,
Unknowing what strange thing might chance him next,
And ere he found fit words to make reply,
The porter bade a youth who stood hard by
Conduct the princely stranger, as was meet,
Through the great golden gate into the street,
And thence o'er all the city, wheresoe'er
Was aught to show of wonderful or fair.

With that the Prince, beside his willing guide,
Went straightway through the gate, and stood inside
The wall, that, builded of a rare white stone,
Clasp'd all the city like a silver zone.
And thence down many a shining street they passed,
Each one appearing goodlier than the last,
Cool with the presence of innumerous trees
And fountains playing before palaces.
And whichsoever way the Prince might look,
Another marvel, and another, took
His wildered eyes with very wonderment.
And holding talk together as they went,
The Prince besought his guide to tell him why
Of all the many folk that passed them by
There was not one that had the looks of eld,
Or yet of life's mid-years ; for they beheld
Only young men and maidens everywhere,
Nor ever saw they one that was not fair.
Whereat the stripling : " Master, thou hast seen,
Belike, the river that doth flow between
Flowers and grasses at the city's feet ? "
And when the Prince had rendered answer meet,
" Then," said the other, " know that whosoe'er
Drinks of the water thou beheldest there
(It matters not how many are his years)
Thenceforward from that moment he appears

Like as he was in youthly days, before
His passèd summers told beyond a score :
And so the people of this land possess
Unto all time their youth and comeliness."

Scarce had his mouth made answer when there rose
Somewhat of tumult, ruffling the repose
Of the wide splendid street ; and lifting up
His eyes, the Prince beheld a glittering troop
Of horsemen, each upon a beauteous steed,
Toward them coming at a gentle speed.
And as the cavalcade came on apace,
A sudden pleasure lit the stripling's face
Who bore him company and was his guide ;
And " Lo, thou shalt behold our queen," he cried, —
" Even the fairest of the many fair ;
With whom was never maiden might compare
For very loveliness ! " While yet he spake,
On all the air a silver sound 'gan break
Of jubilant and many-tongued acclaim,
And in a shining car the bright queen came,
And looking forth upon the multitude
Her eyes beheld the stranger where he stood,
And round about him was the loyal stir :
And all his soul went out in love to her.

But even while her gaze met his, behold,
The city and its marvels manifold
Seemed suddenly removed far off, and placed
Somewhere in Twilight; and withal a waste
Of sudden waters lay like time between;
And over all that space he heard the queen
Calling unto him from her chariot;
And then came darkness.   And the Dream was not.

PART THE SECOND

A FEARFUL and a lovely thing is Sleep,
And mighty store of secrets hath in keep;
And those there were of old who well could guess
What meant his fearfulness and loveliness,
And all his many shapes of life and death,
And all the secret things he uttereth.
But Wisdom lacketh sons like those that were,
And Sleep hath never an interpreter:
So there be none that know to read aright
The riddles he propoundeth every night.

And verily, of all the wondrous things
By potence wrought of mortal visionings
In that dark house whereof Sleep hath the keys —

Of suchlike miracles and mysteries
Not least, meseems, is this among them all :
That one in dream enamourèd should fall,
And ever afterward, in waking thought,
Worship the phantom which the dream hath brought.
Howbeit such things have been, and in such wise
Did that king's son behold, with mortal eyes,
A more than mortal loveliness, and thus
Was stricken through with love miraculous.

For evermore thereafter he did seem
To see that royal maiden of his dream
Unto her palace riding sovranly ;
And much he marvelled where that land might be
That basking lay beneath her beauty's beams,
Well knowing in his heart that suchlike dreams
Come not in idleness but evermore
Are Fate's veiled heralds that do fly before
Their mighty master as he journeyeth,
And sing strange songs of life and love and death.
And so he did scarce aught but dream all day
Of that far land revealed of sleep, that lay
He knew not where ; and musing more and more
On her the mistress of that unknown shore,
There fell a sadness on him, thus to be
Vext with desire of her he might not see

Yet could not choose but long for; till erewhile
Nor man nor woman might behold the smile
Make sudden morning of his countenance,
But likest one he seemed half-sunk in trance,
That wanders groping in a shadowy land,
Hearing strange things that none can understand.
Now after many days and nights had passed,
The queen, his mother well-beloved, at last,
Being sad at heart because his heart was sad,
Would e'en be told what hidden cause he had
To be cast down in so mysterious wise :
And he, beholding by her tearful eyes
How of his grief she was compassionate,
No more a secret made thereof, but straight
Discovered to her all about his dream —
The mystic happy marvel of the stream,
A fountain running Youth to all the land ;
Flowing with deep dim woods on either hand
Where through the boughs did birds of strange song flit :
And all beside the bloomy banks of it
The city with its towers and domes far-seen.
And then he told her how that city's queen
Did pass before him like a breathing flower,
That he had loved her image from that hour.
" And sure am I," upspake the Prince at last,
" That somewhere in this world so wide and vast

Lieth the land mine eyes have inly seen ; —
Perhaps in very truth my spirit hath been
Translated thither, and in very truth
Hath seen the brightness of that city of youth.
Who knows ? — for I have heard a wise man say
How that in sleep the souls of mortals may,
At certain seasons which the stars decree,
From bondage of the body be set free
To visit farthest countries, and be borne
Back to their fleshly houses ere the morn."

   At this the good queen, greatly marvelling,
Made haste to tell the story to the king ;
Who hearing laughed her tale to scorn.   But when
Weeks followed one another, and all men
About his person had begun to say
" What ails our Prince ?   He groweth day by day
Less like the Prince we knew . . . wan cheeks, and
    eyes
Hollow for lack of sleep, and secret sighs . . .
Some hidden grief the youth must surely have," —
Then like his queen the king himself wox grave ;
And thus it chanced one summer eventide,
They sitting in an arbour side by side,
All unawares the Prince passed by that way,
And as he passed, unmark'd of either — they

Nought heeding but their own discourse — could hear
Amidst thereof his own name uttered clear,
And straight was 'ware it was the queen who spake,
And spake of him ; whereat the king 'gan make
Answer in this wise, somewhat angerly :
" The youth is crazed, and but one remedy
Know I, to cure such madness — he shall wed
Some princess ; ere another day be sped,
Myself will bid this dreamer go prepare
To take whom I shall choose to wife ; some fair
And highborn maiden, worthy to be queen
Hereafter." — So the Prince, albeit unseen,
Heard, and his soul rebelled against the thing
His sire had willed ; and slowly wandering
About the darkling pleasance — all amid
A maze of intertangled walks, or hid
In cedarn glooms, or where mysterious bowers
Were heavy with the breath of drowsèd flowers —
Something, he knew not what, within his heart
Rose like a faint-heard voice and said " Depart
From hence and follow where thy dream shall lead.'
And fain would he have followed it indeed,
But wist not whither it would have him go.

Howbeit, while yet he wandered to and fro,
Among his thoughts a chance remembrance leapt

All sudden — like a seed, that long hath slept
In earth, upspringing as a flower at last,
When he that sowed forgetteth where 'twas cast;
A chance remembrance of the tales men told
Concerning one whose wisdom manifold
Made all the world to wonder and revere —
A mighty mage and learn'd astrologer
Who dwelt in honour at a great king's court
In a far country, whither did resort
Pilgrims innumerable from many lands,
Who crossed the wide seas and the desert sands
To learn of him the occult significance
Of some perplexing omen, or perchance
To hear forewhisperings of their destiny
And know what things in aftertime should be.
" Now surely," thought the Prince, " this subtile seer,
To whom the darkest things belike are clear,
Could read the riddle of my dream and tell
Where lieth that strange land delectable
Wherein mine empress hath her dwelling-place.
So might I look at last upon her face,
And make an end of all these weary sighs,
And melt into the shadow of her eyes ! "
Thus musing, for a little space he stood
As holden to the spot ; and evil, good,
Life, death, and earth beneath and heaven above,

Shrank up to less than shadows, — only Love,
With harpings of an hundred harps unseen,
Filled all the emptiness where these had been.

But soon, like one that hath a sudden thought,
He lifted up his eyes, and turning sought
The halls once more where he was bred, and passed
Through court and corridor, and reached at last
His chamber, in a world of glimmer and gloom.
Here, while the moonrays filled the wide rich room,
The Prince in haste put off his courtly dress
For raiment of a lesser sumptuousness
(A sober habit such as might disguise
His royal rank in any stranger's eyes)
And taking in his hand three gems that made
Three several splendours in the moonlight, laid
These in his bosom, where no eye might see
The triple radiance ; then all noiselessly
Down the wide stair from creaking floor to floor
Passed, and went out from the great palace-door.

Crossing the spacious breadth of garden ground,
Wherein his footfalls were the only sound
Save the wind's wooing of the tremulous trees,
Forth of that region of imperial ease

He fared, amid the doubtful shadows dim,
No eye in all the place beholding him ;
No eye, save only of the warders, who
Opened the gates that he might pass therethrough.

And now to the safe-keeping of the night
Intrusted he the knowledge of his flight ;
And quitting all the purlieus of the court,
Out from the city by a secret port
Went, and along the moonlit highway sped.
And himself spake unto himself and said
(Heard only of the silence in his heart)
" Tarry thou here no longer, but depart
Unto the land of the Great Mage ; and seek
The Mage ; and whatsoever he shall speak,
Give ear to that he saith, and reverent heed ;
And wheresoever he may bid thee speed,
Thitherward thou shalt set thy face and go.
For surely one of so great lore must know
Where lies the land thou sawest in thy dream :
Nay, if he know not that, — why, then I deem
The wisdom of exceeding little worth
That reads the heavens but cannot read the earth."

PART THE THIRD

So without rest or tarriance all that night,
Until the world was blear with coming light,
Forth fared the princely fugitive, nor stayed
His wearied feet till morn returning made
Some village all a-hum with wakeful stir;
And from that place the royal wayfarer
Went ever faster on and yet more fast,
Till, ere the noontide sultriness was past,
Upon his ear the burden of the seas
Came dreamlike, heard upon a cool fresh breeze
That tempered gratefully a fervent sky.
And many an hour ere sundown he drew nigh
A fair-built seaport, warder of the land
And watcher of the wave, with odours fanned
Of green fields and of blue from either side; —
A pleasant place, wherein he might abide,
Unknown of man or woman, till such time
As any ship should sail to that far clime
Where lived the famous great astrologer.

Entered within its gates, a wanderer
Besoiled with dust and no-wise richly drest,
Yet therewithal a prince and princeliest

Of princes, with the press of motley folk
He mixed unheeded and unknown, nor spoke
To any, no man speaking unto him,
But, being wearied sore in every limb,
Sought out a goodly hostel where he might
Rest him and eat and tarry for the night :
And having eaten he arose and passed
Down to the wharves where many a sail and mast
Showed fiery-dark against the setting sun :
There, holding talk with whom he chanced upon,
In that same hour by great good hap he found
The master of a vessel outward-bound
Upon the morrow for that selfsame port
Whither he sought to go (where dwelt at court
The mage deep-read in starry charact'ry).
An honest man and pleasant-tongued was he,
This worthy master-mariner ; and since
He had no scorn of well-got gain, the Prince
Agreed to pay him certain sums in gold,
And go aboard his vessel, ere were told
Two hours of sunlight on the coming day ;
And thus agreed they wended each his way,
For the dusk hour was nigh, and all the West
Lay emptied of its sun.   But as he pressed
Up the long seaward-sloping street that ran
Through half the town, the Prince sought out a man

Who dealt in pearls and diamonds and all
Manner of stones which men do precious call ;
To whom the least of his three gems he sold
For a great price, and laden with the gold
Forthwith returned unto his hostelry
And dreamed all night of seaports and the sea.

Early the morrow-morn, a fair soft gale
Blowing from overland, the ship set sail
At turning of the tide ; and from her deck
The Prince gazed till the town was but a speck,
And all the shore became a memory :
And still he gazed, though more he might not see
Than the wide waters and the great wide sky.
And many a long unchangeful day went by
Ere land was sighted, but at length uprose
A doubtful dusky something, toward the close
Of the last hour before one sultry noon :
Most like an isle of cloud it seemed, but soon
The sailors knew it for the wishèd strand,
And ere the evenfall they reached the land,
And that same night the royal wanderer lay
In a strange city, amid strange folk, till Day
Rose from the dim sea's lap and with his wings
Fanned into wakefulness all breathing things.

Then he uprose, but going forth that morn
A sadness came upon him, and forlorn
He felt within himself, and nowise light
Of heart : for all his lonely travel might
Prove void and fruitless and of no avail,
(Thus pondered he) and should it wholly fail,
What then were left him for to do?   Return
To his own country, that his kin might learn
To know him duped and fooled of fantasies,
Blown hither and thither by an idle breeze
From Dreamland?   Or in lieu, perchance, of this,
Wander unresting, reft of hope and bliss,
A mariner on a sea that hath no coast,
Seeking a shade, himself a shade, and lost
In shadows, as a wave is lost i' the sea.

Thus in a heart not lightsome pondered he,
And roamed from unfamiliar street to street,
Much marvelling that all he chanced to meet
Showed faces troubled as his own : for some
Did weep outright, and over all a gloom
Hung, as a cloud that blotteth out the sun.
Wherefore the Prince addressed him unto one
Of sadder visage even than the rest,
Who, ever as he walked, or beat his breast
Or groaned aloud or with his fingers rent

His robe, and, being besought to say what meant
This look of rue on all men's faces, cried
In loud amazement, " What, can any abide
Within this city, having ears to hear,
Yet know not how this morn the mighty seer
Hath died and left the land all desolate?
For now, when sudden ills befall the state,
There will be none to warn or prophesy
As he, but when calamities are nigh
No man will know till they be come and we
Be all undone together, woe is me !"

   Thus ended he his outcry and again
Passed on his way and mixed with other men
Scarce joyfuller than he, if less they spake.
Meanwhile upon the Prince's heart there brake
Grief like a bitter wind, beneath whose breath
Hope paled and sickened well-nigh unto death :
For lo, those dumb and formless fears that came
Within his heart that morn, and, like a flame
That flickers long and dimly ere it die,
Tarried and would not pass, but fitfully
Flickered and flared and paled and flared again, —
Lo, those mysterious messengers of pain,
Dumb formless fears, were they not verified?
And lo, that voyage o'er the waters wide,

Was it not vain and a most empty thing?
And what might now the years avail to bring,
But hopes that barren live and barren die?

Thus did his heart with many an inward sigh
Ask of itself, though answer there was none
To be returned : and so the day, begun
Tristfully, trailed an ever wearier wing ;
Till toward night another questioning
Like a strange voice from far beset his soul :
And as a low wind wails for very dole
About a tarn whereof the listless wave
Maketh no answer to its plaining, save
A sound that seems the phantom of its own,
So that low voice making unbidden moan
No answer got, saving the many sighs
Its echoes ; and in this reproachful wise,
Heaping new pain on him disconsolate,
The low voice spake and spake, importunate :
O Prince that wast and wanderer that art,
Say doth love live within thy hidden heart
(*Love born of dream but nurtured wakingly*)
Ev'n as that Once when thy soul's eyes did see
Love's visible self, and worship?   Or hast thou
Fall'n from thy faith in Her and Love ere now,
And is thy passion as a robe outworn ?

Nay, love forbid! Yet wherefore art thou lorn
Of hope and peace if Love be still thine own?
For, were the wondrous vision thou hast known
Indeed Love's voice and Fate's (which are the same)
Then, even as surely as the vision came,
So surely shall it be fulfilled, if faith
Abide in thee; but if thy spirit saith
Treason of Love or Fate, and unbelief
House in thy heart, then surely shall swift grief
Find thee, and hope (that should be as a breath
Of song undying) shall even die the death,
And thou thyself the death-in-life shalt see,
O Prince that wast, O wanderer that shalt be!

So spake the Voice.   And in the pauses of
That secret Voice, there 'gan to wake and move,
Deep in his heart, a thing of blackest ill —
The shapeless shadow men call Doubt, until
That hour all unacquainted with his soul:
And being tormented sore of this new dole,
There came on him a longing to explore
That sleep-discovered flowery land once more,
Isled in the dark of the soul; for he did deem
That were he once again to dream The Dream,
His faith new-stablishèd would stand, and be
No longer vext of this infirmity.

And so that night, ere lying down to sleep,
There came on him, half making him to weep
And half to laugh that such a thing should be,
A mad conceit and antic fantasy
(And yet more sad than merry was the whim)
To crave this boon of Sleep, beseeching him
To send the dream of dreams most coveted.
And ere he lay him down upon his bed,
A soft sweet song was born within his thought;
But if he sang the song, or if 'twas nought
But the soul's longing whispered to the soul,
Himself knew hardly, while the passion stole
From that still depth where passion lieth prone,
And voiced itself in this-like monotone :

" O Sleep, thou hollow sea, thou soundless sea,
Dull-breaking on the shores of haunted lands,
Lo, I am thine : do what thou wilt with me.

But while, as yet unbounden of thy bands,
I hear the breeze from inland chide and chafe
Along the margin of thy muttering sands,

Somewhat I fain would crave, if thou vouchsafe
To hear mine asking, and to heed wilt deign.
Behold, I come to fling me as a waif

Upon thy waters, O thou murmuring main !
So on some wasteful island cast not me,
Where phantom winds to phantom skies complain,

And creeping terrors crawl from out the sea,
(For such thou hast) — but o'er thy waves not cold
Bear me to yonder land once more, where She

Sits throned amidst of magic wealth untold :
Golden her palace, golden all her hair,
Golden her city 'neath a heaven of gold !

So may I see in dreams her tresses fair
Down-falling, as a wave of sunlight rests
On some white cloud, about her shoulders bare,
Nigh to the snowdrifts twain which are her breasts."

So ran the song, — say rather, so did creep,
With drowsy faltering feet unsure, till Sleep
Himself made end of it, with no rude touch
Sealing the lips that babbled overmuch.
Howbeit the boon of boons most coveted
Withholden was, and in that vision's stead
Another Dream from its dim hold uprose,
Which he who tells the tale shall straight disclose.

PART THE FOURTH

THAT night he dreamed that over him there stole
A change miraculous, whereby his soul
Was parted from his body for a space,
And through a labyrinth of secret ways
Entered the world where dead men's ghosts abide
To seek the Seer who yestermorn had died.
And there in very truth he found the Seer,
Who gazing on him said, " What would'st thou here,
O royal-born, who visitest the coasts
Of darkness, and the dwellings of the ghosts ? "

Then said the Prince, " I fain would know to find
The land as yet untrod of mortal-kind
Which I beheld by gracious leave of Sleep."
To whom the Spirit : " O Prince, the seas are deep
And very wide betwixt thee and that land,
And who shall say how many days do stand,
As dim-seen armèd hosts between thy bliss
And thee ? — Moreover, in the world there is
A certain Emerald Stone which some do call
The Emerald of the Virtues Mystical ;
(Though what those Virtues Mystical may be
None living knows) and since, O youth, to me

Thou dost apply for counsel, be it known
Except thou have this wondrous emerald stone,
Go seek through all the world, thou shalt not find
The land thou wouldst : but like the houseless wind
That roams the world to seek a resting-place,
Thou through inhospitable time and space
Shalt roam, till time and space deliver thee,
To spaceless, timeless, mute eternity.

" For in a certain land there once did dwell
(How long ago it needs not I should tell)
At the king's court a great astrologer,
Ev'n such as erst was I, but mightier
And far excelling ; and it came to pass
That he fell sick ; and very old he was ;
And knowing that his end was nigh, he said
To him that sat in sorrow by his bed,
' O master well-beloved and matchless king,
Take thou and keep this lowly offering
In memory of thy servant ; ' whereupon
The king perceived it was a gem that shone
Like the sea's heart : and on one side of it
This legend in an unknown tongue was writ —
Who holdeth Me may go where none hath fared
Before, and none shall follow afterward.
So the king took the bright green stone betwixt

His fingers, and upon the legend fixed
His eyes, and said unto the dying Seer,
' Now who shall render this dark scripture clear
That I may know the meaning of the gift?'
And the mage oped his mouth and strove to lift
His voice, but could not, for the wishèd word
Clave to his rattling throat, that no man heard :
Whereby the soul, departing, bore away
From all men living, even to this day,
The secret.   And the jewel hath passed down
Seven times from sire to son, and in the crown
It shineth of that country's kings, being called
Ev'n to this day the mystic emerald ;
But no man liveth in the world, of wit
To read the writing that is on it writ."

   " O Master," said the Prince, " and wilt not thou
Instruct me where to find the king who now
Weareth the jewel in his diadem ? "
To whom the Spirit, " O youth, and if the gem
Be worth the finding, is't not also worth
The little pain of seeking through the earth? —
Yet so thou may'st not wander witlessly,
Look thou forget not this I tell to thee :
When in thy journeyings thou shalt dream once more
The fateful dream thou haddest heretofore,

That filled thy veins with longing as with wine,
Till all thy being brimm'd over — by that sign
Thou mayest know thyself at last to be
Within the borders of his empery
Who hath the mystic emerald stone, whose gleam
Shall light thee to the country of thy dream."

"But," said the Prince, "When all the world's high
    ways
My feet have trod, till after length of days
I reach the land where lies the wondrous stone,
How shall I make so rare a thing mine own?
For had I riches more than could be told,
What king would sell his jewels for my gold?"
And on this wise the answer of the Seer
Fell in the hollow of his dreaming ear:
"Behold this Iron Chain, — of power it is
To heal all manner of mortal maladies
In him that wears it round his neck but once,
Between the sun's downgoing and the sun's
Uprising: take it thou, and hold it fast
Until by seeking long thou find at last
The king that hath the mystic emerald stone:
And having found him, thou shalt e'en make known
The virtues lodged within this charmèd chain:
Which when the king doth hear he will be fain

To have possession of so strange a thing ;
And thou shalt make a bargain with the king
To give the Iron Chain in bartery
For that mysterious jewel whereof he
Knows not the secret worth.   And when at last
The emerald stone in thy own hands thou hast,
Itself shall guide thee whither thou would'st go —
Ev'n to the land revealed of sleep, where no
Grief comes to mar their music, neither sound
Of sighing, while the golden years go round."

So spake the Spirit unto him that dreamed,
And suddenly that world of shadow seemed
More shadowy ; and all things began to blend
Together : and the dream was at an end.

Then slept the Prince a deep sweet sleep that knew
Nor dream nor vision ; till the dawnlight grew
Up, and his soul a sudden halt did make
About the confines dim of sleep and wake,
Where wandering lights and wildered shadows meet.
But presently uprising to his feet
From tarriance in that frontier-region dim,
Exceeding wonderment laid hold on him ;
For even while from off his bed he rose,
He heard a clinking as of metal, close

Thereby, and could in no-wise understand :
And lo the Iron Chain was in his hand !

PART THE FIFTH

So, being risen, the Prince in brief while went
Forth to the market-place, where babblement
Of them that bought and them that sold was one
Of many sounds in murmurous union —
A buzzing as of bees about their hives,
With shriller gossiping of garrulous wives
Piping a tuneless treble thereunto :
In midst whereof he went his way as who
Looketh about him well before he buys,
To mark the manner of their merchandise ;
Till chancing upon one who cried for sale
A horse, and seeing it well-limb'd and hale,
And therewithal right goodly to behold,
He bought the beast and paid the man in gold,
And having gotten him the needful gear
Rode from the market, nothing loth to hear
Its garrulous wives no longer, and the din
Of them that daily bought and sold therein.
So from the place he passed, and slowly down
Street after street betook him till the town

Behind him and the gates before him were,
And all without was cornland greenly fair.

And through the cornland wending many a mile,
And through the meadowland, he came erewhile
To where the highways parted, and no man
Was nigh to tell him whitherward they ran ;
But while he halted all in doubtful mood,
An eagle, as if mourning for her brood
Stolen, above him sped with rueful cry ;
And when that he perceived the fowl to fly
Plaining aloud, unto himself he said,
" Now shall yon mournful mother overhead
Instruct the wandering of my feet, and they
Shall follow where she leadeth : " and away
The bird went winging westward clamorously,
That westward even in her wake went he.
And it may be that in his heart there stirred
Some feeling as of fellowship with the bird ;
For he, like her, was bound on a lone quest ;
And for his feet, as for her wings, no rest
Might be, but only urgence of desire,
And one far goal that seemed not ever nigher.

So through that country wended he his way,
Resting anights, till on the seventh day

He passed unwares into another land,
Whose people's speech he could not understand —
A tract o'er-run with tribes barbarian,
And blood-red from the strife of man with man :
And truly 'twas a thing miraculous
That one should traverse all that rude land thus,
And no man rid him of his gold, nor raise
A hand to make abridgment of his days ;
But there was that about him could make men's
Hearts, ere they knew it, yield him reverence, —
Perchance a sovran something in his eye,
Whereat the fierce heart failed, it wist not why ; —
Perchance that Fate which (hovering like a doubt
Athwart his being) hemmed him round about,
Gloomed as a visible shadow across his way,
And made men fearful.   Be this as it may,
No harm befell him in that land, and so
He came at last to where the ebb and flow
Of other seas than he had wandered o'er
Upflung to landward an attempered roar ;
And wandering downward to the beach, he clomb
To topmost of a tall grey cliff, wherefrom
He saw a smoke as of men's houses, far
Off, from a jutting point peninsular
Uprising : whence he deemed that there a town
Must surely be.   And so he clambered down

The cliff, and getting him again to horse
Thither along the seabound held his course,
And reached that city about sunset-tide
The smoking of whose hearths he had espied.

    There at an hostel rested he, and there
Tarried the coming of the morn.   But ere
He fell asleep that night, a wandering thought,
Through darkling byeways of the spirit brought,
Knock'd at his soul for entrance, whispering low
" What if to-night thou dream The Dream, and know
To-morrow, when thou wakest from that bliss,
The land wherein thou liest to be his
Who hath the mystic jewel in his keep ? "
So, full of flattering hope he fell asleep,
And sleeping dreamed, but dreamed not that he would :
For at one time it seemed as if he stood
Alone upon a sterile neck of land,
Where round about him upon either hand
Was darkness, and the cry of a dark sea,
And worldwide vapours glooming thunderously ;
And ever as he stood, the unstable ground
Slid from beneath his feet with a great sound,
Till he could find no foothold anywhere
That seemed not unsubstantial as the air.
At otherwhiles he wandered all alone

About a lonely land, and heard a moan
As of some bird that sang and singing grieved ;
And peering all about the woods thick-leaved
If so he might espy the bird, he found
At length, after long searching, that the sound
Even from the bottom of his own heart came,
And unawares his own mouth sang the same.
And then in dream 'twas like as years went by,
And still he journeyed, hardly knowing why,
Till at the last a mist about him fell,
And if the mist were death he could not tell,
For after that he knew no more.   And so
He slept until the cock began to crow.

Then came the gladful morn, that sendeth sick
Dreams flying, and all shapes melàncholic
That vex the slumbers of the love-distraught.
Unto his heart the merry morning brought
Cheer, and forewhisperings of some far-off rest,
When he should end in sweet that bitter quest.
But going forth that morn, and with his feet
Threading the murmurous maze of street and street,
All strangely fell upon him everywhere
The things he saw and heard of foul or fair.
The thronging of the folk that filled the ways ;
The hubbub of the street and market-place ;

The sound of heavy wain-wheels on the stones ;
The comely faces and ill-favoured ones ;
The girls with apple-cheeks and hair of gold ;
The grey locks and the wrinkles of the old ; —
All these remote and unfamiliar
Seem'd, and himself a something from afar,
Looking at men as shadows on the wall
And even the veriest shadow among them all.

But now when all things dreamwise seemed to swim
About the dubious eyes and ears of him,
That nothing in the world might be believed,
It chanced that on a sudden he perceived
Where one that dealt in jewels sat within
His doorway, hearkening to the outer din,
As who cared no-wise to make fast his ears
Against the babble of the street-farers :
Whereat the merchant, seeing a stranger pass,
Guessed by his garb what countryman he was,
And giving him good-day right courteously
Bespake him in his mother-tongue ; for he
Had wandered in his youth o'er distant seas
And knew full many lands and languages.
Wherefore with him the royal stranger fell
To talking cheerly, and besought him tell
Whence all his gems were had and costly things,

Talismans, amulets, and charmèd rings :
Whereto the other answered, They had come
Some from a country not far hence, and some
From out a land a thousand leagues away
To eastward, ev'n the birthplace of the Day,
The region of the sun's nativity ;
And giving ear to this right readily
The Prince would fain be told of him the way
To that far homeland of the youngling Day.
So, being ask'd, the other answered, " Sir,
There liveth but one master-mariner
Whose ship hath sailed so far : and that is he
Who hither brought the jewels thou dost see.
And now, as luck will have it for the nonce,
He wills to voyage thitherward but once
Before he die — for he is old like me —
And even this day se'nnight saileth he.
Wherefore if thou be fain to see that land,
There needeth only gold within thy hand :
For gold, if that it jingle true and clear,
Hath still a merry music for man's ear,
And where is he that hateth sound of it ? "
So saying, the merchant bade the stranger sit,
But the Prince thanked him for his courtesy,
And went his way.   And that day se'nnight he
Was sailing toward the far-off morningland,

And felt the skies about him like a band,
And heard the low wind uttering numerous noise,
And all the great sea singing as one voice.

PART THE SIXTH

EVEN as one voice the great sea sang. From out
The green heart of the waters round about,
Welled as a bubbling fountain silverly
The overflowing song of the great sea ;
Until the Prince, by dint of listening long,
Divined the purport of that mystic song ;
(For so do all things breathe articulate breath
Into his ears who rightly harkeneth)
And, if indeed he heard that harmony
Aright, in this wise came the song of the sea :

" Behold all ye that stricken of love do lie,
Wherefore in manacles of a maiden's eye
Lead ye the life of bondmen and of slaves?
Lo in the caverns and the depths of Me
A thousand mermaids dwell beneath the waves :
A thousand maidens meet for love have I,
Ev'n I the virgin-hearted cold chaste sea.

Behold all ye that weary of life do lie,
There is no rest at all beneath the sky
Save in the nethermost deepness of the deep.
Only the silence and the midst of Me
Can still the sleepless soul that fain would sleep ;
For such, a cool death and a sweet have I,
Ev'n I the crystal-hearted cool sweet sea.

Behold all ye that in my lap do lie,
To love is sweet and sweeter still to die,
And woe to him that laugheth me to scorn !
Lo in a little while the anger of Me
Shall make him mourn the day that he was born :
For in mine hour of wrath no ruth have I,
Ev'n I the tempest-hearted pitiless sea."

So sang the waters, if indeed 'twere they
That sang unto the Prince's ears that day,
Since in the ship was not a soul besides
Could hear that burden of the voiceful tides ;
For when he told the sailors of this thing,
And ev'n what words the waters seemed to sing,
They stared astonishment, and some, that had
More churlish souls than others, held him mad,
And laughed before his face outright.   But when
The captain heard the gossip of his men

Touching this marvel, the strange news begot
No merry mood in him, who wist not what
Should be the meaning of the miracle,
Nor whether 'twere an omen good or ill.
Wherefore the old seafarer — having heard
The tale retold with many an afterword
The mariners' own most fruitful wit supplied
To grace the telling — took the Prince aside,
And ask'd him sundry questions privily
Concerning this same singing of the sea.
So the Prince told him all there was to tell,
And when that he had heard, the old man fell
To meditating much, and shook his head
As one exceeding ill at ease, and said,
" I doubt the singing thou hast heard was no
Voice of the waters billowing below,
But rather of some evil spirit near,
Who sought with singing to beguile thine ear,
Spreading a snare to catch the soul of thee
In meshes of entangling melody,
Which taketh captive the weak minds of men.
Therefore if thou should'st hear the sound again,
Look thou content thee not with hearkening,
But cast thine eyes around, and mark what thing
Thou seëst, and let no man know but me."

So spake the white-haired wanderer of the sea.
And on the morrow — when the sealine grew
O'erhazed with visible heat, and no wind blew,
And the half-stifled morning dropt aswoon
Into the panting bosom of the noon —
There came into the Prince's ears anew
The song that yestermorn had hearkened to.
And lifting up his eyes in hope to see
What lips they were that made such melody
And filled him with the fulness of their sound,
He saw the sun at highest of his round
Show as a shield with one dark bloodstain blurred,
By reason of the body of some great bird
Like to an eagle, with wide wings outspread,
Athwart the sunfire hovering duskly red.
So to the master of the ship he told
What he had witnessed, bidding him behold
The marvel with his own eyes if he would ;
Who, though he strained his vision all he could,
Yet might not once endure to look the sun
I' the face ; and calling to him one by one
The whole ship's crew, he bade each mariner look
Sunward who could, but no man's eyes might brook
The glare upon them of the noontide rays
And lidless fervour of that golden gaze :
So none of them beheld the bodeful bird.

Then said the greybeard captain, hardly heard
Amid the babble of voices great and small,
" The bird thou seëst is no bird at all,
But some unholy spirit in guise of one ;
And I do fear that we are all undone
If any amongst us hearken to its voice ; —
For of its mouth, I doubt not, was the noise
Thou heardest as of dulcet carolling,
When at thine ear the waters seemed to sing."

And truly, many a wiser man than he
Herein had farther strayed from verity ;
For that great bird that seemed to fan the sun's
Face with its wings was even the same as once
Flew screaming westward o'er the Prince's head,
Beguiling him to follow where it fled.
And bird it was not, but a spirit of ill,
Man-hating, and of mankind hated still,
And slave to one yet mightier demon-sprite
Whose dwelling is the shadow of the night.

So the days passed, and always on the next
The bird-sprite like a baleful vision vexed
The happy-hearted sunlight ; and each time
Its false sweet song was wedded to the rhyme
And chime of wind and wave — although it dropped

As honey changed to music — the Prince stopped
His ears, and would not hear ; and so the Sprite,
Seeing his charmèd songcraft of no might
Him to ensnare who hearkened not at all,
On the tenth day with dreadful noise let fall
A tempest shaken from the wings of him,
Whereat the eyes of heaven wox thunderous-dim,
Till the day-darkness blinded them, and fell
Holding the world in night unseasonable.
And from his beakèd mouth the demon blew
A breath as of a hundred winds, and flew
Downward aswoop upon the labouring bark,
And, covered of the blear untimely Dark,
Clutch'd with his gripple claws the Prince his prey,
And backward through the tempest soared away,
Bearing that royal burden ; and his eyes
Were wandering wells of lightning to the skies.

Long time the Prince was held in swound, and knew
Nor outer world nor inner, as they flew
From darkness unto darkness ; till at last —
The fierce flight over, and his body cast
Somewhere alone in a strange place — the life
Stirred in him faintly, as at feeble strife
With covetous Death for ownership of him.
And 'fore his eyes the world began to swim

All vague, and doubtful as a dream that lies
Folded within another, petal-wise.
And therewithal himself but half believed
His own eyes' testimony, and perceived
The things that were about him as who hears
A distant music throbbing toward his ears
At noontide, in a flowery hollow of June,
And listens till he knows not if the tune
And he be one or twain, or near or far,
But only feels that sound and perfume are,
And tremulous light and leafy umbrage : so
The Prince beheld unknowing, nor fain to know.

About him was a ruinous fair place,
Which Time, who still delighteth to abase
The highest, and throw down what men do build,
With splendid prideful barrenness had filled,
And dust of immemorial dreams, and breath
Of silence, which is next of kin to death.
A weedy wilderness it seemed, that was
In days forepast a garden, but the grass
Grew now where once the flowers, and hard by
A many-throated fountain had run dry
Which erst all day a web of rainbows wove
Out of the body of the sun its love.
And but a furlong's space beyond, there towered

In middest of that silent realm deflowered
A palace builded of black marble, whence
The shadow of a swart magnificence
Falling, upon the outer space begot
A dream of darkness when the night was not.
Which while the Prince beheld, a wonderment
Laid hold upon him, that he rose and went
Toward the palace-portico apace,
Thinking to read the riddle of the place.
And entering in (for open was the door)
From hall to hall he passed, from floor to floor,
Through all the spacious house, and (saving where
The subtile spider had his darksome lair)
No living creature could he find in it.
Howbeit, by certain writing that was writ
Upon the wall of one dark room and bare,
He guessed that some great sorcerer had there
Inhabited, a slave to his own lust
Of evil power and knowledge, till the dust
Received his dust, and darkness had his soul ;
But ere death took him he had willed the whole
Of his possessions to a Spirit of Ill,
His sometime mate in commerce damnable,
Making him lord of that high house, wherein
The twain had sealed their covenant of sin.

With that a horror smote the Prince, and fain
Would he have fled that evil spirit's domain
And shook its dust from off his feet that hour.
But from a window of the topmost tower
Viewing the dim-leaved wilderness without,
Full plainly he perceived it hemmed about
With waves, an island of the middle sea,
In watery barriers bound insuperably ;
And human habitation saw he none,
Nor heard one bird a-singing in the sun
To lighten the intolerable stress
Of utter undisputed silentness.

So by these signs he knew himself the thrall
Of that foul spirit unseen, and therewithal
Wholly unfellowed in captivity,
Bound round with fetters of the tyrannous sea.
And sick for very loneliness, he passed
Downward through galleries and chambers vast
To one wide hall wherefrom a vestibule
Opened into a dim green space and cool,
Where great trees grew that various fruitage bore
The like whereof he had not seen before,
And hard by was a well of water sweet ;
And being anhungered he did pluck and eat
The strange fair fruit, and being athirst did drink

The water, and lay down beside the brink ;
Till sleep, as one that droppeth from the skies,
Dropt down, and made a mist about his eyes.

PART THE SEVENTH

BUT Sleep, who makes a mist about the sense,
Doth ope the eyelids of the soul, and thence
Lifteth a heavier cloud than that whereby
He veils the vision of the fleshly eye.
And not alone by dreams doth Sleep make known
The sealèd things and covert — not alone
In *visions* of the night do mortals hear
The fatal feet and whispering wings draw near ;
But dimly and in darkness doth the soul
Drink of the streams of slumber as they roll,
And win fine secrets from their waters deep :
Yea, of a truth, the spirit doth grow in sleep.

Howbeit I know not whether as he slept
A voice from out the depth of dream upleapt
And whispered in his ear ; or whether he
Grew to the knowledge blindly, as a tree
Waxes from bloom to fruitage, knowing not
The manner of its growth : but this I wot,

That rising from that sleep beside the spring
The Prince had knowledge of a certain thing
Whereof he had not wist until that hour —
To wit, that two contending spirits had power
Over *his* spirit, ruling him with sway
Altern; as 'twere dominion now of Day
And now of Dark; for one was of the light,
And one was of the blackness of the night.

Now there be certain evil spirits whom
The mother of the darkness in her womb
Conceived ere darkness' self; and one of these
Did rule that island of the middle seas
Hemmed round with silence and enchantment dim.
Nothing in all the world so pleasured him
As filling human hearts with dolorousness
And banning where another sprite did bless;
But chiefly did his malice take delight
In thwarting lovers' hopes and breathing blight
Into the blossoms newly-openèd
Of sweet desire, till all of sweet were fled:
And (for he knew what secret hopes did fill
The minds of men) 'twas even now his will
To step between the Prince and his desire,
Nor suffer him to fare one furlong nigher
Unto that distant-shining golden goal
That beacon'd through the darkness to his soul.

And so the days, the sultry summer days,
Went by, and wimpled over with fine haze
The noiseless nights stole after them, as steals
The moon-made shadow at some traveller's heels.
And day by day and night by night the Prince
Dwelt in that island of enchantment, since
The hour when Evil Hap, in likeness of
An eagle swooping from the clouds above,
Did bind him body and soul unto that place.
And in due time the summer waxed apace,
And in due time the summer waned : and now
The withered leaf had fallen from the bough,
And now the winter came and now the spring ;
Yea, summer's self was toward on the wing
From wandering overseas : and all this while
The Prince abode in that enchanted isle,
Marvelling much at Fortune and her ways.

And by degrees the slowly-sliding days
Gathered themselves together into years,
And oftentimes his spirit welled in tears
From dawn to darkness and from dark to dawn,
By reason of the light of life withdrawn.
And if the night brought sleep, a fitful sleep,
The phantoms of a buried time would creep
Out of their hollow hiding-places vast,

Peopling his Present from the wizard Past.
Sometimes between the whirl of dream and dream,
All in a doubtful middle-world, a gleam
Went shivering past him through the chill grey space,
And lo he knew it for his mother's face,
And wept ; and all the silence where he stood
Wept with him.   And at times the dreamer would
Dream himself back beneath his father's roof
At eventide, and there would hold aloof
In silence, clothed upon with shadows dim,
To hear if any spake concerning him ;
But the hours came and went and went and came,
And no man's mouth did ever name his name.
And year by year he saw the queen and king
Wax older, and beheld a shadowy thing
Lurking behind them, till it came between
His dreamsight and the semblance of the queen,
From which time forth he saw her not : and when
Another year had been it came again,
And after that he saw his sire the king
No more, by reason of the shadowy thing
Stepping between ; and all the place became
As darkness, and the echo of a name.

    .   .   .   .   .   .

What need to loiter o'er the chronicle
Of days that brought no change ? What boots it tell

The tale of hours whereof each moment was
As like its fellow as one blade of grass
Is to another, when the dew doth fall
Without respect of any amongst them all?
Enow that time in that enchanted air
Nor slept nor tarried more than otherwhere,
And so at last the captive lived to see
The fiftieth year of his captivity.
And on a day within that fiftieth year
He wandered down unto the beach, to hear
The breaking of the breakers on the shore,
As he had heard them ofttimes heretofore
In days when he would sit and watch the sea,
If peradventure there some ship might be.
But now his soul no longer yearned as then
To win her way back to the world of men :
For what could now his freedom profit him?
The hope that filled youth's beaker to its brim
The tremulous hand of age had long outspilled,
And whence might now the vessel be refilled?
Moreover, after length of days and years
The soul had ceased to beat her barriers,
And like a freeborn bird that cagèd sings
Had grown at last forgetful of her wings.

And so he took his way toward the sea —
Not, as in former days, if haply he

Might spy some ship upon the nether blue,
And beckon with his hands unto the crew,
But rather with an easeful heart to hear
What things the waves might whisper to his ear
Of counsel wise and comfortable speech.
But while he walked about the yellow beach,
There came upon his limbs an heaviness,
For languor of the sultry time's excess ;
And so he lay him down under a tree
Hard by a little cove, and there the sea
Sang him to sleep.   And sleeping thus, he dreamed
A dream of very wonderment : himseemed,
The spirit that half an hundred years before
In likeness of an eagle came and bore
His body to that island on a day,
Came yet again and found him where he lay,
And taking him betwixt his talons flew
O'er seas and far-off countries, till they drew
Nigh to a city that was built between
Four mountains in a pleasant land and green ;
And there upon the highest mountain's top
The bird that was no bird at all let drop
Its burthen, and was seen of him no more.

Thereat he waked, and issuing from the door
Of dream did marvel in his heart ; because

He found he had but dreamed the thing that was :
For there, assuredly, was neither sea
Nor Isle Enchanted ; and assuredly
He sat upon the peak of a great hill ;
And far below him, looking strangely still,
Uptowered a city exceeding fair to ken,
And murmurous with multitude of men.

PART THE EIGHTH

Now as it chanced, the day was almost spent
When down the lonely mountain-side he went,
The whitehaired man, the Prince that was ; and ere
He won the silence of the valley where
The city's many towers uprose, the gate
Was closed against him, for the hour was late.
So even as they that have not wherewithal
To roof them from the rain if it should fall,
Upon the grassy ground this king's son lay,
And slept till nigh the coming of the day.

But while as any vagabond he slept
Or outcast from the homes of men, there crept
Unto him lying in such sorry sort
A something fairer than the kingliest court

In all the peopled world had witness of —
Even the shadow of the throne of Love,
That from a height beyond all height did creep
Along the pavement of the halls of sleep.
O fair and wonderful ! that shadow was
The golden dream of dreams that came across
His youth, full half an hundred years before,
And sent him wandering through the world.   Once
    more
In a lone boat that sails and oars had none,
Midmost a land of summer and the sun
Where nothing was that was not fair to see,
Adown a gliding river glided he,
And saw the city that was built thereby,
And saw the chariot of the queen draw nigh,
And gazed upon her in the goodly street ;
Whereat he waked and rose upon his feet,
Remembering the Vision of the Seer,
And what the spirit spake unto his ear :
" When in thy wanderings thou shalt dream once more
The fateful dream thou haddest heretofore,
That filled thy veins with longing as with wine
Till all thy being brimm'd over — by that sign
Thou mayest know thyself at last to be
Within the borders of his empery
Who hath the mystic emerald stone, whose gleam
Shall light thee to the country of thy dream."

Then rose the heart within his heart and said :
" O bitter scornful Fate, in days long dead
I asked and thou denied'st mine asking : now
The boon can no-wise profit me, and thou
Dost mock me with bestowal ! "   Thereupon
He fell to thinking of his youthhood gone,
And wept.   For now the goal, the longtime-sought,
Was even at hand, " but how shall I," he thought,
" I that am old and sad and hoary-haired,
Enter the place for youth and love prepared ?
For in my veins the wellspring of desire
Hath failed, and in mine heart the golden fire
Burneth no more for ever.   I draw near
The night that is about our day, and hear
The sighing of the darkness as I go
Whose ancient secret there is none doth know."

Ev'n so to his own heart he spake full sad,
And many and bitter were the thoughts he had
Of days that were and days that were to be.
But now the East was big with dawn, and he
Drew nigh the city-gates and entered in,
Ere yet the place remurmured with the din
Of voices and the tread of human feet ;
And going up the void and silent street,
All in the chill gleam of the new-lit air,

A Thought found way into his soul, and there
Abode and grew, and in brief while became
Desire, and quickened to a quenchless flame :
And holding converse with himself, he said,
" Though in my heart the heart's desire be dead,
And can no more these time-stilled pulses move ;
Though Death were lovelier to these eyes than Love
Yet would these eyes behold, or ere I pass,
The land that mirror'd lay as in a glass
In the deep wells of dream.   And her that is
The sunlight of that city of all bliss,
Her would I fain see once with waking eyes
Whom sleep hath rendered unto vision twice.
And having seen her beauty I would go
My way, even to the river which doth flow
From daylight unto darkness and the place
Of silence, where the ghosts are face to face."

So mused the man, and evermore his thought
Gave him no peace.   Wherefore next morn he sought
The palace of the king, but on his way
Tarried till nigh the middle of the day
In talk with certain of the city-folk ;
Whereby he learned, if that were true they spoke,
How that the king their lord was nigh distract
With torture of a strange disease that racked

Each day his anguished body more and more,
Setting at naught the leeches and their lore.
Which having heard he went before the king,
Who sat upon his throne, delivering
Judgment, his body pierced the while with pain.
And taking from his neck the charmèd chain
Which he had borne about him ever since
That morn miraculous, the unknown Prince
Upspake and said, " O king, I hold within
My hand a wonder-working medicine
Of power to make thee whole if thou wilt deign
So to be healèd ; " and he held the chain
Aloft, and straightway told unto the king
The passing worth and wonder of the thing.

 Then he that heard stretched forth a hand that
  shook
With sudden fever of half-hope, and took
The chain, and turned it over in his hand
Until his eyes had left no link unscanned.
And on each separate link was character'd
A language that no living ear had heard,
Occult, of secret import, mystic, strange.
Then said the king, " What would'st thou in exchange
For this the magic metal thou dost bring ? "
And the Prince answered him and said, " O king,

Even the emerald stone which some do call
The Emerald of the Virtues Mystical."
And they who thronged the hall of judgment were
Astonished at the stranger who could dare
Ask such a boon ; and some base mouths did curl
With sneers, churl whispering to his fellow churl,
" Who could have deemed the man so covetous,
So void of shame in his great greed ? "   For thus
It shall be ever underneath the sun,
Each man believing that high hearts are none
Whose own is as the dust he treads on low.

But the king answered saying, " Be it so.
To-night this chain of iron shall be worn
About my neck, and on the morrow-morn,
If all the pain have left these limbs of mine,
The guerdon thou demandest shall be thine.
But if this torment still tormenteth me,
Thy head and shoulders shall part company,
And both be cast uncoffin'd to the worms.
Open thy mouth and answer if these terms
Content thee."   And aloud the Prince replied,
" With these conditions I am satisfied : "
Whereafter, rising from his knees, he went
Out from before the king, and was content.

Next morning, when the king awoke, I wis
No heart was lighter in the land than his;
For all the grievous burden of his pains
Had fall'n from off his limbs, and in his veins
Upleapt the glad new life, and the sick soul
Seemed like its body all at once made whole.
But hardly was the king uprisen before
There knock'd and entered at the chamber-door
His chief physician (a right skilful leech,
But given to hollow trickeries of speech,
And artful ways and wiles) who said, "O king,
Be not deceived, I pray thee. One good thing
Comes of another, like from like. The weed
Beareth not lilies, neither do apes breed
Antelopes. Thou art healèd of thy pain
Not by the wearing of an iron chain —
An iron chain forsooth!" — (hereat he laughed
As 'twere a huge rare jest) "but by the draught
Which I prepared for thee with mine own hands
From certain precious simples grown in lands
It irks me tell how many leagues away :
Which medicine thou tookest yesterday."

Then said the king, "O false and jealous man,
Who lovest better thine own praises than
Thy master's welfare ! Little 'tis to such

As thou, that I should be made whole ; but much
That men should go before thee, trumpeting
" ' Behold the man that cured our lord the king.' "
And he was sore displeased and in no mood
To hearken.   But the chief physician stood
Unmoved amid this hail of kingly scorn,
With meek face martyr-like, as who hath borne
Much in the name of Truth, and much can bear.
And from the mouth of him false words and fair
So cunningly flowed that in a little while
The royal frown became a royal smile,
And the king hearkened to the leech and was
Persuaded.   So that morn it came to pass
That when the Prince appeared before the throne
To claim his rightful meed, the emerald stone,
The king denied his title to receive
The jewel, saying, " Think'st thou I believe
Yon jingling chain hath healed my body?   Nay ;
For whatsoever such as thou may say
I am not found so easy to beguile :
As for the gem thou wouldest, this good while
It hath adorned the crown I wear, nor shall
The stone be parted from the coronal."

     Scarce had the false king spoken when behold
Through the high ceiling's goodly fretted gold

A sudden shaft of lightning downward sped
And smote the golden crown upon his head,
Yea, melted ev'n as wax the golden crown.
And from the molten metal there fell down
A grassgreen Splendour, and the Emerald Stone
Tumbled from step to step before the throne,
And lay all moveless at the Prince's feet !
And the king sat upon his royal seat
A dead king, marble-mute : but no man stirred
Or spake : and only silence might be heard.

Then he before whose feet the gem did lie
Said not a word to any man thereby, .
But stooped and lifted it from off the floor,
And passing outward from the open door
Put the mysterious jewel in his breast
And went his way, none daring to molest
The stranger.   For the whisper rose and ran,
" Is not the lightning leaguèd with this man ? "

PART THE NINTH

AND passing through the city he went out
Into the fat fields lying thereabout,
And lo the spirit of the emerald stone
With secret influence to himself unknown

Guided the wandering of his errant feet,
The servants of the errant soul; and sweet
The meadows were, with babble of birds, and noise
Of brooks, the water's voice and the wind's voice.
Howbeit he gave small heed to any of them;
And now the subtile spirit of the gem
Led him along a winding way that ran
Beyond the fields to where the woods began
To spread green matwork for the mountains' feet;
A region where the Silence had her seat
And hearkened to the sounds that only she
Can hear — the fall of dew on herb and tree;
The voice of the growing of the grass; the night
Down-fluttering breathless from the heaven's height;
And autumn whispering unawares at times
Strange secrets and dark sayings, wrapt in rhymes
Wind-won from forest branches.   At this place
The old man rested for a little space,
Forgetful that the day was wellnigh flown:
But soon the urgent spirit of the stone
Itself re-entered and possessed anew
His soul; and led thereby, and wandering through
A mile of trackless and untrodden ground,
By favour of the rising moon he found
A rude path, broken here and there by rills
Which crossed it as they hurried from the hills.

And going whitherso the wild path went,
A two hours' journeying brought him, wellnigh spent
With toiling upwards, to a mountain pass,
A bleak lone place where no trees grew nor grass,
But on each hand a peak of rock, high-reared,
Uprose : afar the two like horns appeared
Of some great beast, so tapering-tall they were.
And now with forward gaze the wanderer
Stood where the pass was highest and the track
Went downward both ways ; and behind his back
The full moon shone, and lo before his face
The bright sea glimmered at the mountain's base.
It seemed, what way soever he might turn,
His fate still led him to that watery bourn.

So journeying down the track which lay before,
He came, an hour past midnight, to the shore,
And, looking backward, far above espied
The two sharp peaks, one peak on either side
Of that lone pass ; verily like a pair
Of monstrous horns, the tips far-seen, up there :
And in the nether space betwixt the two,
A single monstrous eye the moon shone through.

Now all this while the spirit of the stone
Had led him forward, he, the old man lone,

Taking no thought of whither he was bound.
And roaming now along the beach he found
A creek, and in the creek, some little way
From where it joined the sea, a pinnace lay
Moored at the marge ; and stepping thereinto,
He sat him down, and from his bosom drew
The mystic gem, and placed it at the prow,
That he might watch its paly splendours, how
They lightened here and there, and flashed aflame,
Mocked at the moon and put the stars to shame.
But hardly was the stone out of his hand,
When the boat wrenched her moorings from the land,
And swift as any captive bird set free
Shot o'er the shimmering surface of the sea,
The spirit of the emerald guiding her ;
And for a time the old man could not stir
For very greatness of astonishment.

But merrily o'er the moonlit waters went
The pinnace, till the land was out of sight,
Far in the dreaming distance.   All that night,
Faster than ever wind in winter blew,
Faster than quarrel flies the bow, she flew.
A moment was a league in that wild flight
From vast to vast of ocean and the night.
And now the moon her lanthorn had withdrawn :

And now the pale weak heralds of the dawn
Lifted the lids of their blear eyes afar :
The last belated straggler of a star
Went home ; and in her season due the morn
Brake on a cold and silent sea forlorn —
A strange mute sea, where never wave hath stirred,
Nor sound of any wandering wind is heard,
Nor voice of sailors sailing merrily :
A sea untraversed, an enchanted sea
From all the world fate-folden ; hemmed about
Of linkèd Dreams ; encompassed with a Doubt.

But not the less for lack of wind went she,
The flying pinnace, o'er that silent sea,
Till those dull waters of enchantment lay
Behind her many a league.   And now her way
Was toward a shining tract of ocean, where
Low winds with bland breath flattered the mild air,
And low waves did together clasp and close,
And skyward yearning from the sea there rose
And seaward yearning from the sky there fell
A Spirit of Deep Content Unspeakable :
So midway meeting betwixt sky and sea,
These twain are married for eternity,
And rule the spirits of that Deep, and share
The lordship of the legions of the air.

Here winds but came to rest them from their wars
With far seas waged.   Here Darkness had her stars
Always, a nightly multitudinous birth.
And entering on this happier zone of earth,
The boat 'gan bate her speed, and by degrees
Tempered her motion to the tranquil seas,
As if she knew the land not far ahead,
The port not far : so forward piloted
By that sweet spirit and strong, she held her way
Unveering.   And a little past midday,
The wanderer lifted up his eyes, and right
Before him saw what seemed a great wall, white
As alabaster, builded o'er the sea,
High as the heaven ; but drawing nearer he
Perceived it was a mighty mist that lay
Upon the ocean, stretching far away
Northward and southward, and the sun appeared
Powerless to melt its mass.   And while he neared
This cloudy barrier stretching north and south,
A tale once told him by his mother's mouth,
In childhood, while he sat upon her knee,
Rose to remembrance : *how that on the sea*
Sat somewhere a Great Mist which no sun's heat
Could melt, nor wind make wander from its seat.
So great it was, the fastest ship would need
Seven days to compass it, with all her speed.

And they of deepest lore and wisest wit
Deemed that an island in the midst of it
Bloomed like a rosebush ring'd with snows, a place
Of pleasance, folded in that white embrace
And chill. But never yet would pilot steer
Into the fog that wrapped it round, for fear
Of running blindfold in that sightless mist
On sunken reefs whereof no mariner wist:
And so from all the world this happy isle
Lay hidden. Thus the queen, long since ; and while
He marvelled if the mist before his ken
Could be the same she told of — even then,
Hardly a furlong 'fore the pinnace' prow
It lay : and now 'twas hard at hand : and now
The boat had swept into the folds of it !
But all that vision of white darkness — lit
By the full splendour of the emerald stone
That from the forepart of the pinnace shone —
Melted around her, as in sunder cleft
By that strong spirit of light ; and there was left
A wandering space, behind her and before,
Of radiance, roofed and walled with mist, the floor
A liquid pavement large. And so she passed
Through twilight immemorial, and at last
Issued upon the other side, where lay
The land no mortal knew before that day.

There wilding orchards faced the beach, and bare
All manner of delicious fruit and rare,
Such as in gardens of kings' palaces
Trembles upon the sultry-scented trees,
The soul of many sunbeams at its core.
Well-pleased the wanderer landed on this shore,
Beholding all its pleasantness, how sweet
And soft, to the tired soul, to the tired feet.
And so he sat him down beneath the boughs,
And there a low wind seemed to drone and drowse
Among the leaves as it were gone astray
And like to faint forwearied by the way ;
Till the persistence of the sound begat
An heaviness within him as he sat :
So when Sleep chanced to come that way, he found
A captive not unwilling to be bound,
And on his body those fine fetters put
Wherewith he bindeth mortals hand and foot.

When the tired sleeper oped again his eyes,
'Twas early morn, and he beheld the skies
Glowing from those deep hours of rest and dew
Wherein all creatures do themselves renew.
The laughing leaves blink'd in the sun, throughout
Those dewy realms of orchard thereabout ;
But green fields lay beyond, and farther still,

Betwixt them and the sun, a great high hill
Kept these in shadow, and the brighter made
The fruitlands look for all that neighbouring shade.
And he the solitary man uprose,
His face toward the mountain beyond those
Fair fields not yet acquainted with the sun ;
And crossed the fields, and climbed the hill, and won
The top ; and journeying down the eastern side
Entered upon a grassy vale and wide,
Where in the midst a pure stream ran, as yet
A youngling, hardly able to forget
The lofty place of its nativity,
Nor lusting yet for union with the sea.
And through this valley, taking for his guide
The stream, and walking by the waterside,
He wandered on, but had at whiles to ford
The lesser brooks that from the mountains poured
Into this greater ; which by slow degrees,
Enlarged with such continual soft increase,
Became a river broad and fair, but still
As clear as when it flowed a mountain-rill :
And he the wanderer wandering by that stream
Saw 'twas the river he had known in dream.

So day by day he journeyed ; and it chanced
One day he fared till night was well advanced

Ere lying down to sleep ; and when he waked
Next morn, his bones and all his body ached,
And on his temples lay a weary heat,
And with sore pain he got upon his feet.
Yet when he rose and hard at hand espied
The City sloping to the riverside,
With bright white walls and golden port agleam,
Such as he saw them figured in the dream —
Then the blood leapt as fire along his veins
And the o'erwearied limbs forgat their pains.
But when he strove to make what speed he might
Toward the happy haven full in sight,
The feet that would have hastened thereunto
Could not ; and heavily, as old men do,
He fell to earth, and groaned aloud and said,
" Old man, what would'st thou, with thy silvered head,
Yonder, where all their tresses be as gold
For ever? — Thou art suffered to behold
The city of thy search : what wilt thou more?
Tarry thou here upon this river-shore ;
Thou mightest farther go nor find the grass
Greener, whereon to lay thy head, and pass
Into the deep dark populous empty land."

So spake the man, not able to withstand
This dumb remonstrance of the flesh, now first

Thwarting the soul.   Howbeit a mighty thirst
Consumed him, and he crawled unto the brink
Of the clear stream hard by, that he might drink
One draught thereof, and with the water still
His deep desire.   When lo a miracle !
No sooner had he drunken than his whole
Body was changed and did from crown to sole
The likeness of its youthful self put on,
The Prince of half-an-hundred years agone,
Wearing the very garments that he wore
What time his years were but a single score.

   Then he remembered how that in The Dream
One told him of the marvel of that stream,
Whose waters are a well of youth eterne.
And night and day its crystal heart doth yearn
To wed its youthhood with the sea's old age ;
And faring on that bridal pilgrimage,
Its waters past the shining city are rolled,
And all the people drink and wax not old.

PART THE TENTH

THAT night within the City of Youth there stood
Musicians playing to the multitude
On many a gold and silver instrument
Whose differing souls yet chimed in glad consent.
And sooth-tongued singers, throated like the bird
All darkness holds its breath to hear, were heard
Chanting aloud before the comely folk,
Chanting aloud till none for listening spoke,
Chanting aloud that all the city rang ;
And whoso will may hear the song they sang : —

I

" O happy hearts, O youths and damsels, pray
What new and wondrous thing hath chanced to-day,
O happy hearts, what wondrous thing and new?
Set the gold sun with kinglier-mightful glance,
Rose the maid-moon with queenlier countenance,
Came the stars forth a merrier madder crew,
Than ever sun or maiden-moon before,
Or jostling stars that shook the darkness' floor
With night-wide tremor 'neath their dizzy dance?

Strong is the Sun, but strong alway was he;
The Moon is fair, but ever fair showed she;
The Stars are many, and who hath known them few?
As now they be, so heretofore were they:
What is the wondrous thing hath chanced to-day,
O happy hearts, the wondrous thing and new,
Whereof ye are glad together even more
Than of the sunlight or the moonlight or
The light o' the stars that strow the milky-way?

For all your many maidens have the head
In goodly festal wise engarlanded,
With flowers at noon the banquet of the bees,
And leaves that in some grove at midday grew:
And ever since the falling of the dew
Your streets are full of pomps and pageantries,
Laughter and song, feasting and dancing: — nay,
Surely some wondrous thing hath chanced to-day;
O happy hearts, what wondrous thing and new?

II

No, no, ye need not answer any word!
Heard have we all — who lives and hath not heard? —
What thing the sovran Fates have done to-day;
Who turn the tides of life which way they please,

And sit themselves aloft, aloof, at ease :
Dwellers in courts of marble silence they.
No need to ask what thing the Fates have done
Between the sunrise and the set of sun,
Mute-moving in their twilight fastnesses !

Changeless, aloft, aloof, mute-moving, dim,
In ancient fastnesses of twilight — him
Have they not sent this day, the long-foretold,
The long-foretold and much-desired, of whom
'Twas whilom written in the rolls of doom
How in a dream he should this land behold,
And hither come from worldwide wandering,
Hither where all the folk should hail him king,
Our king foredestined from his mother's womb?

Long time he tarried, but the time is past,
And he hath come ye waited for, at last :
The long-foretold, the much-desired, hath come.
And ye command your minstrels noise abroad
With lyre and tongue your joyance and his laud,
And, sooth to say, the minstrels are not dumb.
And ever in the pauses of our chant,
So for exceeding perfect joy ye pant,
We hear the beating of your hearts applaud !

III

And she our Queen — ah, who shall tell what hours
She bode his coming in her palace-towers,
Unmated she in all the land alone?
'Twas yours, O youths and maids, to clasp and kiss;
Desiring and desired ye had your bliss:
The Queen she sat upon her loveless throne.
Sleeping she saw his face, but could not find
Its phantom's phantom when she waked, nor wind
About her finger one gold hair of his.

Often when evening sobered all the air,
No doubt but she would sit and marvel where
He tarried, by the bounds of what strange sea;
And peradventure look at intervals
Forth of the windows of her palace walls,
And watch the gloaming darken fount and tree;
And think on twilight shores, with dreaming caves
Full of the groping of bewildered waves,
Full of the murmur of their hollow halls.

As flowers desire the kisses of the rain,
She his, and many a year desired in vain:
She waits no more who waited long enow.
Nor listeth he to wander any more

Who went as go the winds from sea to shore,
From shore to sea who went as the winds go.
The winds do seek a place of rest ; the flowers
Look for the rain ; but in a while the showers
Come, and the winds lie down, their wanderings o'er

VITA NUOVA

Long hath she slept, forgetful of delight :
At last, at last, the enchanted princess, Earth,
Claimed with a kiss by Spring the adventurer,
In slumber knows the destined lips, and thrilled
Through all the deeps of her unageing heart
With passionate necessity of joy,
Wakens, and yields her loveliness to love.

O ancient streams, O far-descended woods
Full of the fluttering of melodious souls ;
O hills and valleys that adorn yourselves
In solemn jubilation ; winds and clouds,
Ocean and land in stormy nuptials clasped,
And all exuberant creatures that acclaim
The Earth's divine renewal : lo, I too
With yours would mingle somewhat of glad song.
I too have come through wintry terrors, — yea,
Through tempest and through cataclysm of soul
Have come, and am delivered. Me the Spring,
Me also, dimly with new life hath touched,

And with regenerate hope, the salt of life ;
And I would dedicate these thankful tears
To whatsoever Power beneficent,
Veiled though his countenance, undivulged his thought,
Hath led me from the haunted darkness forth
Into the gracious air and vernal morn,
And suffers me to know my spirit a note
Of this great chorus, one with bird and stream
And voiceful mountain, — nay, a string, how jarred
And all but broken ! of that lyre of life
Whereon himself, the master harp-player,
Resolving all its mortal dissonance
To one immortal and most perfect strain,
Harps without pause, building with song the world.

APRIL 16TH 1893.

LYRIC LOVE.

An Anthology.

EDITED BY

WILLIAM WATSON.

(With a steel vignette after Stoddard, engraved by W. Ridgway.)

Golden Treasury Series, 16mo, $1.00. Also in Ornamental Silk, $1.50 ; Half Morocco, $3.00.

MACMILLAN & CO.,

112 FOURTH AVENUE, NEW YORK.

THE DEATH OF ŒNONE,

AKBAR'S DREAM, *and* OTHER POEMS

BY

ALFRED LORD TENNYSON.

16mo. $1.25.

A few Copies of the limited large Paper Edition are still for sale. Price, $3.00.

" ' Œnone ' is of singular beauty — that ' excellent beauty ' noted by Bacon, which has in it something ' strange.' It is very brief; but its very brevity, stern and strong, gives it a greater force. . . . Since Dido fell upon her love-less pyre, few statelier scenes of love's death have been portrayed in this Virgilian manner." — *The Academy.*

" There is as much of sadness as of pleasure in the feeling with which one takes up this new volume of poems. It is the swan-song of a great poet; with two or three exceptions, the book is entirely new. There is some rare music in it, and some songs that none but he could have sung." — *Chicago Tribune.*

WANDERERS.

Being a collection of the Poems of WILLIAM WINTER. New edition, revised and enlarged. With a Photogravure Portrait of the author. Limited large paper edition, printed on English hand-made paper. Price, $2.50.

" . . . But it has seemed to the author of these poems — which of course are offered as absolutely impersonal — that they are the expression of various representative moods of human feeling and various representative aspects of human experience, and that therefore they possibly possess the inherent right to exist." — *From the Preface.*

" The poems have a singular charm in their graceful spontaneity." — *Scots Observer.*

" Free from cant and rant — clear-cut as a cameo, pellucid as a mountain brook. It may be derided as trite, *borné*, unimpassional; but in its own modest sphere it is, to our thinking, extraordinarily successful, and satisfies us far more than the pretentious mouthing which receives the seal of over-hasty approbation." — *Athenæum.*

MACMILLAN & CO.,
112 FOURTH AVENUE, NEW YORK.